Thou Therefore My Son...

Training The Lord's Servant

By

Dick York

i

The message of this book is available on MP3 CD and can be purchased from SOF Publications at the address below.

Other available titles by the same author in print and CD:
Law's End: The Galatian Letter
Truth or Tradition, Does it Matter?
God's Eternal Purpose: The Making of Man in God's Image
I Will Build My Church: The Ephesian Letter

© 2008 All Rights Reserved
ISBN 978-1-889575-06-3

SOF Publications
296 NE Alpenview Lane
Bend, Oregon 97701

Phone (541) 330-6684
Email: sofpublications@sfmiusa.org

Contents

Foreword   iv

Introduction to Warfare   9

That Good Thing Keep   17

Endure Hardness as a Good Soldier   33

Unentangled   57

Suffering, Resurrection and Reward   69

Rightly Dividing the Word   79

Perilous Times   95

Preach The Word   107

Defection and Discipleship   115

Independence   121

Foreword

The Apostle Paul summed up his ministry in unequivocal terms when, in Ephesians 5:32, he stated simply, *"I speak concerning Christ and the church"*

From the time that Paul, blinded and numbed by the sobering vision on the Damascus road, met Ananias, confirmed his commitment to Christ and began to meet with the believers in Damascus,[1] his walk with the Lord was a walk with the Lord's people. When he left Damascus for Jerusalem, he immediately *"assayed to join himself to the disciples"* [2] and when the initial roadblocks to fellowship were taken away, he was *"with them coming in and going out at Jerusalem."*[3] After a hiatus in Tarsus, we find Paul assembling with the church in Antioch and teaching many.[4] When he was called to an apostolic ministry, he dedicated himself for perhaps forty years to establishing and strengthening churches in new areas and charging those churches to multiply throughout their region.[5] Of the thirteen Pauline epistles we have, nine are written to local congregations.

For Paul, to love and serve the Lord Jesus meant, love and serve the church.

On his second missionary journey, he was reacquainted with a young man named Timothy whom he had lead to Christ on his initial visit through Galatia. Time has passed and now, when Paul returned to the region, he found a zealous young man, fervent in his love for Christ and the church. Timothy's testimony was known in his home town of Lystra and in the town of Iconium, eighteen miles away. While eighteen miles may not seem much today, one wonders what it cost Timothy to travel by foot, donkey or on horseback to visit the congregation of Iconium. Paul was impressed by this young man and desired him to come along on the missionary journey he was undertaking. The elders of the church being in agreement, Paul and the elders laid hands on him, prayed for him, and the church sent him out under Paul's authority.[6]

Thus began a life-long friendship and partnership, with Paul discipling Timothy both by word and by deed, while Timothy served

Paul in errands of increasing responsibility. The relationship of discipler to disciple became one of father to son, and Paul was able to say these stunning words when he spoke of Timothy to the Philippians:

"But I trust in the Lord Jesus to send Timotheus shortly unto you, that I also may be of good comfort, when I know your state. For I have no man like-minded, who will naturally care for your state. For all seek their own, not the things which are Jesus Christ's. But ye know the proof of him, that, as a son with the father, he hath served with me in the gospel."

Note that phrase: *"I have no man like-minded, who will naturally care for your state."*

To be like-minded with the Apostle Paul meant to give oneself body, soul and spirit to building up the church of Jesus Christ, that God might receive the maximum glory. Paul had once listed the difficulties and trials he endured in exercising his apostolic ministry, ending the long list of sufferings by adding, *"Beside those things that are without, that which cometh upon me daily, the care of all the churches."*[7] Timothy, after years at the Apostle Paul's side, naturally—genuinely, faithfully, sincerely—cared for the state of the churches.

Paul is now "Paul the aged", and he writes to his most faithful disciple and, apart from Christ Himself, his dearest friend. A single word, appearing six times in 1 Timothy, sets the theme for both these epistles. That word is *"paragello"*, which means "to transmit a message along from one to another", [8] "to hand on an announcement from one to another."[9] In Paul's letters to Timothy, it is often translated in the King James as a charge:

1 Tim. 1:3 - "...that thou mightest charge some that they teach no other doctrine."

1 Tim. 1:18 - "This charge I commit unto thee, son Timothy..."

1 Tim. 5:7 - "And these things give in charge..."

1 Tim. 5:21 - "I charge thee before God, and the Lord Jesus Christ..."

1 Tim. 6:13 - "I give thee charge in the sight of God..."

1 Tim. 6:17 - "Charge them that are rich in this world, that..."

This word appears more in his first letter to Timothy than in any other of Paul's letters. Clearly, Paul is giving a charge to Timothy. From a wealth of experience and fellowship with the Lord, Paul is handing on a message, charging his son in the faith to fight the good fight.[10]

It is Paul passing the baton.

In a time when heresy was pouring into the church of Jesus Christ, when Paul's message was being set aside by people who wanted rather to have their ears tickled;[11] when preaching the good news was seen as a way to personal wealth, and riches were touted as evidence of faith;[12] when even the most basic doctrines of the faith were being questioned or abandoned;[13] the Apostle turns to his dear friend and disciple and charges him: "Thou therefore my son..." While the first letter toTimothy contains various charges, the second epistle seems to major on just one, expressed in various ways but all returning to the basic challenge: Be strong.

"Stir up the gift..." (1:6), "Be not ashamed..." (1:8), "Hold fast..." (1:13), "That good thing which was committed unto thee keep..." (1:14), "Be strong..." (2:1) ...commit... endure... strive... labor... consider... remember... study... flee... instruct... continue... preach... and so on.

The order. The command. The charge.

That charge which Paul passed to Timothy has, by the grace and protection of God, survived to be passed on to us. We have the Apostle's charge, with all of its authority and power. We, too, are in a time when the straightforward teaching of the Scripture is being set aside by some who seem to desire only to have their ears tickled, when wealth is held out as evidence of spirituality and when basic teachings of the Bible are being rejected by professing believers, even by Christian leaders. This is a time to allow the words of the Apostle Paul, given by inspiration of the Holy Spirit, to drive down deep into our hearts. The church of Jesus Christ in many parts of the world is in danger, and those who love Christ and His people cannot do better than to read, study, learn and apply the epistles written to

Timothy.

By means of the book which you hold in your hands, Dick York, in an engaging and readable style, walks us through Paul's final exhortations to Timothy. With concise explanation and clear application, he brings Paul's final charge into the circumstances and conditions of our day.

This is a charge. A charge to you, to me and to the Body of Christ.

Will we take up that charge?

Please read this book carefully and prayerfully. Hear the Apostle Paul charging you to be strong, to fight the good fight and to "consider what I say and the Lord give you understanding in all things."[14]

Steve Montgomery
President,
Shield of Faith Mission International
June, 2008

(Endnotes)
[1] Acts 9:10-19
[2] Acts 9:26
[3] Acts 9:28
[4] Acts 11:26
[5] 2 Corinthians 10:13-16
[6] 1 Timothy 4:14; 2 Timothy 1:6
[7] 2 Corinthians 11:28
[8] Thayers
[9] Vines
[10] 1 Timothy 6:12; 2 Timothy 4:7
[11] 2 Timothy 4:3
[12] 1 Timothy 6:3-5
[13] 2 Timothy 2:18
[14] 2 Timothy 2:7

Introduction to Warfare

Since the beginning of time, has there been a generation without war? It would seem that in spite of man's unceasing search for peace, and all the promises that politicians make concerning it, war is the normal state. Why is that? Is it because man has no capacity to promote and maintain amicable relationships? Is there something amiss in his character that he likes war?

It seems doubtless that there is something amiss, but even so there are few that like war, especially among those who have experienced it. Civil War General William T. Sherman said, "War is hell." Franklin D. Roosevelt stated with vehemence, "I hate war." These were men who declared war, and conducted war. No man who has experienced war or heard the groaning of the wounded loves war; but he is without power to stop it. It is built into the human heart. The apostle James asks the question,

> *"From whence come wars and fightings among you?*

and answers it,

> *"Come they not hence, even of the lusts that war in your members? Ye lust, and ye have not: ye kill, and desire to have, and cannot obtain: ye fight and war, yet ye have not, because ye ask not. Ye ask, and receive not, because ye*

*ask amiss, that ye may consume it upon your lusts. Ye adul-
terers and adulteresses, know ye not that the friendship of
the world is enmity with God? Whosoever therefore will be
a friend of the world is an enemy of God."* [1]

The problem, obviously, lies in the human heart, and it is called
"sin." Ever since the fall of mankind, this imbedded sin problem has
made man a part of the world system, which is ruled over by God's
arch enemy, Satan, and every member of that system has been enlisted to militate against God's authority. The world is at war!

*"The wicked are like the troubled sea, when it cannot
rest, whose waters cast up mire and dirt. There is no peace,
saith my God, to the wicked."* [2]

The only promise for peace in any generation is in the person of
the Lord Jesus Christ, who is the Prince of Peace. He cries out to a
war-weary world,

*"Come unto me, all ye that labor and are heavy laden,
and I will give you rest. Take my yoke upon you, and learn
of me; for I am meek and lowly in heart: and ye shall find
rest unto your souls. For my yoke is easy, and my burden
is light."* [3]

Those who have come to him for rest have discovered peace
with God. They are no longer engaged in the bone-wearying, mind-
numbing conflict of an unwinnable war against the God who created them for himself. They have come home. They are enjoying
an inward peace that the world could not give.[4] But, often to their
surprise, they soon learn that even his enduring peace is not the
same as the absence of war. Despite the indescribably peaceful rest
that engulfs their inner man, outwardly there is incessant warfare
all around. Whereas once they were a part of the world, in turmoil
and at war with God, now they are in God and the world is at war
with them. The warfare is endless, but now through this reversal of
allegiance they are on the victor's side.

That invitation to come and rest includes an unimaginable transformation that makes the comer to Christ a new creature with everlasting citizenship in an eternal city whose builder is God. While that transformation is as immediate as a birth, and those who have received that heavenly citizenship are at once at peace with God, actual passage to the glorious city is a certain but future hope. In the meantime, those who are now in the Body of Christ, the Church, are a select contingent of people, no longer a part of the world even though they are still in it.[5] Doesn't that mean then that we are now in hostile territory behind enemy lines? And is not spiritual warfare every bit as real and as dangerous as natural warfare?

That's the part about which not all of God's people are persuaded. Many are convinced that the day they believed in the Lord Jesus, because they received citizenship in heaven, the war is over; they own no part in the battle into which they have been unwittingly born. As a consequence, they seem quite comfortable feeding at the world's table, drinking the world's wine and partaking of the world's "good life" fraternizing with the enemy. The result is an overwhelming casualty rate. Especially among their children, who are unprepared for the battle and even, in some cases, unaware that all around them there is a war in progress. So they are swallowed up and taken captive by their "friendly" enemy—captured by, recruited into and trained for the world's army to fight against the God that their parents, because they are members of a church, profess to serve.

"Church" means "called out." Not only are the saints called out of the world, but they are bound together into what should be a formidable company, armed and ready to do battle. Is that inconsistent with the character of God's church as portrayed in scripture? Are they not said to be armed with weapons of warfare?[6] Did not the apostle Paul command believers to "put on the whole armor of God that ye may be able to stand against the wiles of the devil?"[7] Why? Because we wrestle—we fight, we do battle—we are at war!

Doesn't it seem like an oxymoron to be at peace and at war at the same time?

It does.

If peace meant only pleasant circumstances and outward tran-

11

quility; and war meant only "confused noise and garments rolled in blood" as Isaiah the prophet described it, then indeed it would be a contradiction; but there is such a thing as peace in war for those whose trust is in the Lord.

War, in this case, is a battle for the mind and for the soul and even for the bodies of those who are not yet partakers of eternal life, and is meant by the enemy for the destruction of those that are. Peace, on the other hand, is independent of circumstances; it is an undisturbable solace emanating from the presence of the Lord.

> *"Thou wilt keep him in perfect peace whose mind is stayed on thee: because he trusteth in thee."* [8]

There is no circumstance that can annul that promise.

The church, those who have been redeemed out of the world by the blood of the Lord Jesus Christ, are called "living stones" [9] and they are built together to be the temple of the Lord.[10] God promised to dwell in them and walk in them, and that he would be their God and they would be his people.[11] So the church is a single disciplined unit; a house that God lives in, a vehicle he moves in, "the clothes that God wears to work." [12] In other words, the saints are not left to their own devices, nor do they do their own thing independent of the Lord's design.

> *"For it is God which worketh in you both to will and to do of his good pleasure."* [13]

The church, as a body, has a specific commission from the Lord to accomplish in the earth.[14] In order that it might perform according to God's will, he gave clear written instructions through gifted apostles. Then he placed in oversight of each assembly of believers––**and every believer is to be a part of one of these**—two or more mature believers (elders) to guide and guard and maintain order.

Did you ever stop to consider how closely the noun "disciple" resembles the adjective "disciplined"? An army without discipline is simply a mob. A mob, on the other hand, if disciplined and directed, becomes an army able, as a unit, to accomplish the purpose for which it was assembled. The church is not a mob; it is meant to be a company of disciples, ready to carry out God's assigned commission. The instructions that govern the behavior and work of the saints are set forth in the letters written by the apostles to the various churches that comprise our New Testament.

Beside the apostle Paul, several other authors, inspired by the Holy Spirit, contributed to the content of the New Testament. These include the apostles Matthew, Peter, James and John; as well as the medical doctor Luke, John Mark, and the Lord's brother, Jude. Their writings make up the manual for the operation of the churches and instruction for every facet of Christian living.

Do you need counsel for your marriage? It's there in the New Testament as well as in the Old. Do we need to know how to relate to our families; to our wives or husbands? That's there too. What about our friends, or our enemies, or to civil government, or to the authority of the elders? It's there. Also included is prophetic insight into the end times and instruction about the coming kingdom and about heaven; as well as the wretched state of the lost, and the clear revelation of the Gospel. In short, the scriptures include everything we need for life and godliness: including the lowdown on our enemy and how to be victorious in the warfare.

Thirteen of the letters that make up this volume are Paul's epistles. Nine of them are written to the churches; each one dealing with specific issues that encompass every problem and circumstance that occurs in the church today. Do you think the problems of today are different than those that Paul confronted? Actually the problems never change, nor do the solutions. For that reason the Word that God inspired these men to write never ceases to be adequate to address every contemporary circumstance.

There are men that have altered the words, or reinterpreted their meaning with the view of making it more compatible with modern times and customs. This they have done to the peril of today's believers. The truths of God's word are timeless. *Jesus Christ is the same yesterday and today and forever,*[15] as is God. Being perfect and changeless, the word of God will not conform to our customs or our preferences; rather we are to conform to it. Would it not seem logical and fitting to a sea faring man that he must adjust his course according to his compass, rather than changing his compass to suit his present heading?

But not all of Paul's letters were addressed to churches; four of them were written to individuals. Through reading these men's mail we receive the instruction that he gave to them, and it is indispensable, affording us information about the qualifications required for men to be overseers of congregations, and what their duties are. It is instruction that is often ignored or adjusted: but when it is, the church suffers and her testimony is blemished. In these personalized epistles he also deals with character issues, warns of personal pitfalls, and of men who are or will be enemies of the church.

One of Paul's letters to Timothy, his young coworker, is unique in its content. Whereas his other writings deal with the church, and the relationship of its many members to God's word, to each other, and to church authority, this one is an exhortation to personal strength and integrity. In the other letters it seems that the warfare is a collective effort in which the body of believers acts in concert:

> *"In whom* [Christ] *all the building fitly framed together groweth into an* [singular] *holy temple in the Lord: in whom ye* [collective] *also are builded together for an* [singular] *habitation of God through the Spirit."* [16]

> *"That there should be no schism in the body; but that the members should have the same care one for another. And whether one member suffer, all the members suffer with it; or one member be honored, all the members rejoice with it. Now ye* (collective) *are the body of Christ , and members in particular."* [17]

We have compared the church to a great army, disciplined and armed. Can an army be effective in any other mode? Of course not. All of its members must fight as one man. To do that, every soldier must be individually committed to excellence, to obedience and to personal sacrifice. To train an army, you must train the individuals that make up that army. A unit is not properly equipped unless each soldier in it is equipped. A soldier must be dedicated to the objective of the campaign; and that dedication must remain intact even if his fellow soldiers are killed, or wounded—or defect.

When Paul wrote his second letter to Timothy, this seems to be the case. It is Paul's last communication with his faithful junior partner and fellow soldier. He was soon to be ushered in to glory. In this, his last epistle, we gain an insight into the things that he thought important to utter as his last words to a brave comrade-in-arms. We understand from reading Timothy's mail the kind of loyalty, patience, purity, steadfastness, wisdom, integrity and courage a servant of the Lord is admonished to exhibit in circumstances favorable or adverse.

In the chapters that follow, we will peruse the entire second epistle of Paul to Timothy and comment briefly on its content. The text of the letter is printed in ***bold Italics***. Read, absorb, and commit.

(Endnotes)
[1] James 4:1-4
[2] Isaiah 57:20,21
[3] Matthew 11:28,29
[4] John 16:27
[5] John 17:11, 14-16
[6] 2 Corinthians 10:4-6
[7] Ephesians 6: 11, 12
[8] Isaiah 26:3
[9] 1 Peter 2:5
[10] Ephesians 2:21,22
[11] 2 Corinthians 6:16
[12] A quote by Major Ian Thomas, founder of Capernwray Fellowship.
[13] Philippians 2:13
[14] Matthew 28:19,20
[15] Hebrews 13:8
[16] Ephesians 2:21,22
[17] 1 Corinthians 12:25-27

Chapter 1

That Good Thing Keep

1 Paul, an apostle of Jesus Christ by the will of God, according to the promise of life which is in Christ Jesus,

It has been a long haul from Tarsus to this Roman dungeon in which Paul now finds himself imprisoned; and in which he will live out the few remaining days of his life on earth. Listening to the footsteps of his guards and meditating on the faithfulness and goodness of God over the thirty-five plus years since he had been that young man at whose feet the martyr Stephen's executioners had lain their coats, he remembered how he had, shortly thereafter, been struck to the ground in the glare of a light brighter than the noon-day sun. As though it were still ringing in his ears he could hear that voice––*"Saul, Saul, why persecutest thou me?"* And in response to his terrified question, *"Who art thou Lord?"* the answer that captured him forever: *"I am Jesus whom thou persecutest."*

How long ago that had been, and yet how little time seems to have transpired. Thirty-five years—more than half a lifetime—had gone by, carrying the history of this man's involvement in the early church into a glorious past. He recalled the blindness that had resulted from the brilliance of that light, and the man Ananias, whom

God had sent to heal his eyes, and to baptize him, and to tell him what things he must suffer for Jesus' name's sake. [1]

Yes, it was true; since that time he had suffered much for Jesus' sake. Had he not, some years ago, in a letter written to the church at Corinth in their time of rebellion, chronicled a partial list of the sufferings that had accompanied his being an apostle? He could remember well the defense he had made to them of his apostleship when they had been inclined to defect from the truth and follow false teachers, imposters, who claimed to be apostles.

> *"Such are false apostles,"* he wrote, *"deceitful workers, transforming themselves into the apostles of Christ. And no marvel; for Satan himself is transformed into an angel of light...I speak as concerning reproach, as though we had been weak, Howbeit whereinsoever any is bold, (I speak foolishly) I am bold also. Are they Hebrews? So am I. Are they Israelites? So am I. Are they the seed of Abraham? So am I. Are they ministers of Christ? (I speak as a fool) I am more; in labors more abundant, in stripes above measure, in prisons more frequent, in deaths oft. Of the Jews five times received I forty stripes save one. Thrice was I beaten with rods, once was I stoned, thrice I suffered shipwreck, a night and a day have I been in the deep; in journeyings often, in perils of waters, in perils of robbers, in perils by mine own countrymen, in perils by the heathen, in perils in the city, in perils in the wilderness, in perils in the sea, in perils among false brethren; in weariness and painfulness, in watchings often, in hunger and thirst; in fastings often, in cold and nakedness. Beside those things that are without, that which cometh upon me daily, the care of all the churches. Who is weak and I am not weak? Who is offended, and I burn not? If I must needs glory, I will glory in the things that concern mine infirmities...And [the Lord] said to me, 'My grace is sufficient for thee; for my strength is made perfect in weakness.' Most gladly therefore will I rather glory in my infirmities, that the power of Christ*

18

may rest upon me. Therefore I take pleasure in infirmities, in reproaches, in necessities, in persecutions, in distresses for Christ's sake: for when I am weak, then am I strong. I am become a fool in glorying; ye have compelled me; for I ought to have been commended of you: for in nothing am I behind the very chiefest apostles, though I be nothing. Truly the signs of an apostle were wrought among you in all patience, in signs and wonders and mighty deeds." [2]

For many years he had served the Lord as the apostle Christ had called him to be; preaching the gospel, enduring much persecution, surviving great trials, suffering many imprisonments: and all the while demonstrating incredible peace and joy as though he were already in the kingdom of God. Now, it seemed, he was experiencing his final incarceration. In a matter of days, if things ended as it now appeared they would, Paul's head would roll at the hand of one of Nero's executioners. For Paul, the war was over. The trials would soon end; he would have to defend his apostleship no more. For the church, however, the battle would still rage on.

Paul had taught many young men over the course of years; but not all had stood. Whoever would press on in the work would have to, above all, be faithful. Paul had already taken pen in hand to write to the young protégé closest to his heart.

2 *To Timothy, my dearly beloved son: grace, mercy and peace, from God the Father and Christ Jesus our Lord.*

Lystra was Timothy's home town. Stirring memories were invoked when Paul thought of that Lycaonian city. Some twenty-two years ago—about the year AD forty-six—when Paul and Barnabas had first gone to the province of Lycaonia,

"There sat a certain man at Lystra, impotent in his feet, being crippled from his mother's womb, who never had walked: the same heard Paul speak: who steadfastly beholding him, and perceiving that he had faith to be healed,

said with a loud voice, 'Stand upright upon thy feet.' And
he leapt and walked. And when the people saw what Paul
had done, they lifted up their voices in the speech of Lycaonia, 'The gods are come down to us in the likeness of
men.' And they called Barnabas Jupiter; and Paul Mercu-
rius, because he was the chief speaker." Then the priest of
Jupiter, which was before their city, brought oxen and gar-
lands unto the gates, and would have done sacrifice with
the people." ³

It was with great effort that Paul and Barnabas had restrained the
people's worship of them, but it was an opportunity to point them
to the true God. How quickly their adulation had been turned to
frenzied hatred when certain Jews from Antioch and Iconium, who
hated Paul for his defection from Phariseeism, and for the gospel he
now preached, came on the scene and persuaded the people to stone
Paul. They dragged his body out of the city and left him for dead.

But Paul wasn't dead; nor was his ministry to Lystra over. As
some of those who had believed the message stood around his apparently lifeless body, he rose up and returned to the city. The next
day he departed with Barnabas to Derbe.

"And when they had preached the gospel to that city,
and had taught many, they returned again to Lystra, Iconium and Antioch, confirming the souls of the disciples, and
exhorting them to continue in the faith, and that we must,
through much tribulation enter into the kingdom of God." ⁴

A devout Jewess named Lois was among the number who believed. Her daughter Eunice, married to a Greek, was also among
the believers, and Eunice's son Timothy was probably a ten-year-old
when this intrusion of the gospel upon the pagan lifestyle of Lystra
had convulsed their city. It would be approximately seven years before Paul came again to the city of Lystra.

Timothy, nurtured by the faith of his mother and his grandmother and encouraged to continue in the word of God, had grown from
a child to a young man perhaps forty years Paul's junior. His mother

and grandmother had taught him, even as a youngster, the importance of a reputation for maturity and godliness. Do not the scriptures teach that "*Even a child is known by his doings, whether his work be pure, and whether it be right*"? [5]

As all young men should, Timothy had taken this to heart. He was known to be a godly fellow and had a good report among the brethren that were at Lystra and Iconium.

> "*Him would Paul have to go forth with him; and took and circumcised him because of the Jews that were in those quarters: for they knew all that his father was a Greek.*" [6]

Paul may have marveled at the willingness of this young man to subject himself to the discomfort and a degree of humiliation that would accompany the ritual of circumcision. Especially when it wasn't required for any better standing before God; there were no "points" to be gained. In fact Paul would later say when writing to the Galatians, "*If ye be circumcised Christ shall profit you nothing...neither circumcision availeth anything, nor uncircumcision; but faith which worketh by love.*" [7] Timothy had understood that; he knew that this was not for any personal gain. In fact, it was not about him at all, but for the furtherance of the gospel they would preach. It was to diminish inhibition to the reception of the gospel on the part of the Jews to whom they would preach it. Why would the preaching of an uncircumcised "Jew" be credible to a Jew that had embraced the covenant of circumcision? If they perceived his uncircumcision as a despising of Moses' law, would they not despise his gospel message? For this reason he had done it for Jesus' sake; his commitment was total.

> **3 I thank God, whom I serve from my forefathers with pure conscience, that without ceasing I have remembrance of thee in my prayers night and day; 4 greatly desiring to see thee, being mindful of thy tears, that I may be filled with joy 5 when I call to remembrance the unfeigned love that is in thee, which dwelt first in thy**

grandmother Lois, and thy mother Eunice; and I am persuaded that in thee also.

It seems incredible that Paul would recall his life as being, from his forefathers, one of service to God with pure conscience, since he had been such a rabid persecutor of the church. He had already discussed this with Timothy in a previous letter in which he wrote,

"And I thank Christ Jesus our Lord, who hath enabled me, for that he counted me faithful, putting me in the ministry; who was before a blasphemer, and a persecutor, and injurious: but I obtained mercy, because I did it ignorantly and in unbelief, And the grace of our Lord was exceeding abundant with faith and love which is in Christ Jesus. This is a faithful saying, and worthy of all acceptation, that Christ Jesus came into the world to save sinners; of whom I am chief. Howbeit for this cause I obtained mercy, that in me first Jesus Christ might show forth all longsuffering, for a pattern to them which should hereafter believe on him to life everlasting." [8]

God saw Saul's faithful heart, his eagerness to please Him even in his ignorance and unbelief, and his readiness to repent when it would be revealed to him what and who the truth is. There was even more than that: Jesus Christ would reveal in Paul's life a pattern for all believers that should come after him.

Paul knew his own heart; he knew that even as Saul, he was motivated by a sincere religious zeal which, because it was misguided and without the Spirit of God, made him the chiefest of sinners. His sincerity could not alter that, but the longsuffering of Jesus Christ did. Now every sinner, no matter how vile, can see the pattern of God's justifying grace, the absolute transforming power of his redemption, and the separation to his calling that it produces.

6 Wherefore I put thee in remembrance that thou stir up the gift of God, which is in thee by the putting on of my

hands. **7** *For God hath not given us the spirit of fear; but of power, and of love, and of a sound mind.* **8** *Be not thou therefore ashamed of the testimony of our Lord, nor of me his prisoner: but be thou partaker of the afflictions of the gospel according to the power of God;* **9** *Who hath saved us, and called us with an holy calling, not according to our works, but according to his own purpose and grace, which was given us in Christ Jesus before the world began,* **10** *But is now made manifest by the appearing of our Savior Jesus Christ, who hath abolished death, and hath brought life and immortality to light through the gospel:* **11** *Whereunto I am appointed a preacher, and an apostle, and a teacher of the Gentiles.*

For over fifteen years now, Timothy had been Paul's companion in labor. Paul had recognized God's gift to Timothy and communicated that by the laying on of his hands enabling him to minister with confidence. Timothy had observed Paul's zeal, his single-minded purpose to make Christ known, and his willingness to confront danger and to sacrifice all. Now he witnessed the reaction of Rome. For the second time Nero's police had apprehended Paul: the first time to release him after two years of house arrest; this time with the obvious intent to extinguish his light forever.

This is a nerve-shattering event for those closely identified with this high-priority enemy of the state. Obviously, they are on the same government list. Some of Paul's friends and colleagues will defect for their own safety. It is evident to Paul that even Timothy probably wrestled with the temptation to follow that same course. It has been said that courage is not being without fear, but rather staying the course in spite of it.

"Remember your gift, and stir it up," Paul writes, "Because the spirit of fear isn't from God. He gives us the spirit of power, and of love, and of a sound mind."

The enemy's work is to intimidate the saints, to make them tremble before the apparent power of the state or whoever else the opposing forces might be. The fear of death or of defeat causes potential conquerors to turn tail and run away from certain victory. It caused Peter to deny that he knew Jesus; three times he denied him because he was ashamed of the testimony of the Lord. At times like these, if saving our flesh is our purpose, it is probably expedient to be ashamed of those imprisoned for their faith in order to avoid a similar end. Some may even boast that they stay out of trouble by minding their own business, keeping their mouth shut and therefore not making enemies. An anonymous poet penned a verse about that:

> "He has no enemies you say?
> My friend, your boast is poor:
> He that has mingled in the fray
> Of duty that the brave endure
> Must have made foes. If he has none,
> Small is the work that he has done.
> He has hit no traitor on the hip:
> He has cast no cup from tempted lip,
> He has never turned the wrong to right.
> He has been a coward in the fight." [9]

If accomplishing the will of God—defeating the adversary, achieving the victor's crown and glorifying the name of Jesus—is our purpose; then there is no other course than to unashamedly partake of the afflictions of the gospel through the power of God. How can one who is truly a "disciple indeed" walk the path of blessing and reward—and sometimes light affliction—for fifteen years and, in the end defect, despise the climax of the battle and forfeit the reward?

No, Timothy, Jesus saved us, and called us with an holy calling. He didn't call us according to our works, but according to His own purpose and grace. This is something we need to know going into this war. If we are His disciples, if we have come into difficult, even life-threatening circumstances through bold obedience to God's leading, it is His purpose and it is by His grace. He who purposed to commit us to this travail by grace will also, one way or another, deliver us from it by grace; or He will give strength to endure it by grace according to His own will. Let's not forget that *"Unto you it is given in the behalf of Christ, not only to believe on him, but also to suffer for his sake."* [10]

> *"God's purpose and grace was given us in Christ Jesus before the world began, but is now made manifest by the appearing of our Savior Jesus Christ."*

We know that Jesus had a history before he ever appeared on the stage of time. His eternal life as the Word of God is just that— eternal. The apostle John told us that Christ *is* that eternal life. He doesn't just *have* eternal life, He *is* eternal life. Therefore *"He that hath the Son hath life, and he that hath not the son of God hath not life."* [11] To some of us, those words may simply comprise a Bible verse; but that was not the case with Paul. He understood it; he had insight into the eternal nature of the life he had. It motivated him, stabilized him in the face of destabilizing odds; emboldened him in the face of intimidating foes; gave him absolute hope in the face of totally hopeless circumstances.

What was he seeing that made him so unshakably committed? Christ hath abolished death! Why would he fear what God has abolished? Paul understood the gospel; and through the gospel, Christ has brought life and immortality to light. "They can kill me, but I can't die. That's what immortality means. Life is eternal." That's what Jesus taught, but sometimes we are slow to hear and to understand, *"Whosoever liveth and believeth in me shall never die."* It was this that Paul was appointed, as an apostle and preacher, to teach the Gentiles. He would teach it ultimately by his attitude in the coming final day before his executioner.

12 *For the which cause I also suffer these things; nevertheless I am not ashamed: for I know whom I have believed, and am persuaded that he is able to keep that which I have committed unto him against that day.*

Afraid? Of what?
To feel the spirit's glad release?
To pass from pain to perfect peace,
The strife and strain of life to cease?
Afraid? Of that?

Afraid? Of what?
Afraid to see the Savior's face,
To hear His welcome, and to trace,
The glory gleam from wounds of grace,
Afraid? Of that?

Afraid? Of what?
A flash–a crash–a pierced heart;
Brief darkness–Light–O Heaven's art!
A wound of His a counterpart!
Afraid? Of that?

Afraid? Of what?
To enter into Heaven's rest,
And yet to serve the Master blessed?
From service good to service best?
Afraid? Of that?

Afraid? Of what?
To do by death what life could not–
Baptize with blood a stony plot,
Till souls shall blossom from the spot?
Afraid? Of that? [12]

Many heroes of the faith preceded Paul on that course to martyr-
dom; and many since have followed him there. Not all of them were
heroic characters before they were called upon to surrender their
lives, but as God promised, *"As thy day, so shall thy strength be,"*[13]

all of them found his promise true.

Before Paul, that list of heroes of the faith was recorded in Hebrews 11, and many others whose names are not recorded except in heaven. After him came a seemingly endless list of men and women whose lives have been offered up for the sake of lost multitudes in every land. Perhaps the collective sentiment of all of them was best expressed in contemporary terms by the twenty-seven year old husband and father, Jim Elliot, who, as a missionary, gave up his life for a primitive tribe of Ecuadorian Indians. While still in college he wrote, *"**He is no fool who gives what he cannot keep to gain what he cannot lose**."*

> Jesus said, *"For whosoever will save his life shall lose it; but whosoever shall lose his life for my sake and the gospel's, the same shall save it."* [14] And *"Except a corn of wheat fall into the ground and die, it abideth alone: but if it die, it bringeth forth much fruit."* [15]

13 Hold fast the form of sound words, which thou hast heard of me, in faith and love which is in Christ Jesus. 14 That good thing which was committed unto thee keep by the Holy Ghost which dwelleth in us.

Timothy must be convinced, as you and I must be convinced, as Paul is convinced, that everything that is committed to God, He is able to keep. Paul, while he is instructing Timothy, is not speaking theological theory: his persuasion is not being recited from memory out of a catechism; these are his last words—heartfelt, important. He is passing the banner. This is not Paul's war only, nor will it end with his death. It is Timothy's war too, and ours as well. It is the commitment of everyone who deems himself to be a disciple of the Lord Jesus Christ. It didn't end with Paul or the twelve apostles of the Lord Jesus.

The instruction is to hold fast the form of sound words, which we have heard of Paul. That was Timothy's commission. He wasn't

27

just to "hang in there." He had a special trust. Paul, later in this same epistle, makes it clear that *"all scripture is given by inspiration of God, and is profitable for doctrine, for reproof, for correction, for instruction in righteousness."* That which is inspired by God must be preserved and used as God intended it to be used. It is our only weapon in this warfare, and it is effective when it is "rightly divided." For over fifteen years Timothy had shared the ministry with Paul. He had been inspired and no doubt, from time to time, reproved and instructed in righteousness, "Don't deviate from that application of the word that you have seen me demonstrate."

Yes, the Word is our weapon. But we don't use our weapon as the Roman soldiers were taught to use theirs. Force tinged with hatred and violence is the manner of this worlds combat. Timothy had heard the word from Paul in faith and love which is in Christ Jesus. He was to deliver it in the same manner.

"That good thing" which was committed unto Timothy may have been much more than we understand. Only Timothy was privy to the many hours of private talks and encouraging interludes that must have enriched the years of discipling and being discipled that had characterized their relationship. He had been dispatched by Paul to teach the saints and to resolve disputes in the churches; he had been entrusted with complex duties and the appointment of overseers. He had been a surrogate "Paul" on many occasions. Surely the continuation of the ministering of Paul's team was at least part of "that good thing." Timothy's responsibilities in representing the gospel in a despicably dark and dangerous world would continue on, as do ours if we claim to be disciples of the Lord Jesus. Neither could Timothy nor can we keep those commitments except by the power of the Holy Ghost. How encouraging to know that the same Holy Ghost that dwelt in the apostle Paul also dwelt in Timothy…and dwells in us. Paul knew that. *"That good thing keep by the Holy Ghost which dwelleth in us."*

15 *This thou knowest, that all they which are in Asia be turned away from me; of whom are Phygellus and Her-*

> *mogenes. 16 The Lord give mercy unto the house of One-siphorus; for he oft refreshed me, and was not ashamed of my chain; 17 But when he was in Rome, he sought me out very diligently, and found me. 18 The Lord grant unto him that he find mercy of the Lord in that day: and in how many things he ministered unto me at Ephesus, thou knowest very well,*

Keeping our commitments or keeping that which is committed to us is not always a team sport. There are times when we walk through the valley of the shadow of death; and when we do, it will likely be alone. Timothy was observing this. The crowd, even the good ones, had turned away when their support was the most needed and they could have served best. Even men like Onesiphorus who had in the past proven faithful and diligent, had their limits. Timothy was seeing that faithfulness and commitment are personal values that stand on their own foundation, and usually without encouragement from the majority.

For missionary service, Paul was the pattern. As a true disciple of Jesus Christ, Paul was an example. Many have followed that example and brought great blessing through their committed lives and service. It seems, however, that in any given crowd of believers, at any given time, when the committed should be the norm, they are in the minority.

> **2:1 *Thou therefore, my son, be strong in the grace that is in Christ Jesus.***

It had no doubt been a great disappointment to Paul to see so many of his stalwarts turn aside under the pressure of the threat of persecution. Understand, this is no idle threat. The Roman Senate had recently voted almost unanimously not to make legal the new and "troublesome" Christian sect. Shortly after that vote Rome suffered a devastating fire that consumed seventy percent of the city. The despised Christians have been blamed for the conflagration and severe persecution had been the result. In public events organized at the remaining amphitheater, accused Christians, after the manner of a major sporting event, are fed to lions for the amusement of the frenzied crowd of bloodthirsty spectators. Those that do not face the lions are impaled on poles and ignited as human torches. Or, escaping that brutal torture, others are, more humanely, beheaded. The Roman government, which, in effect, is the government of the world, is indeed an intimidating foe. It turned the timid back easily and the strong less easily, but nonetheless it had turned them back. The number left standing is few indeed. For this reason, Paul's exhortation to Timothy—and to us—is an imperative injunction: "Be strong!" Since it is a command, it can be carried out, but only as we stand in the grace of God. What a time to remember that Jesus promised, *"Lo, I am with you always, even to the end of the world."*

(Endnotes)
[1] Acts 9:10-16
[2] 2 Corinthians 11:13-30; 12:9-12
[3] Acts 14:8-13
[4] Acts 14:21,22
[5] Proverbs 20:11
[6] Acts 16:1-3
[7] Galatians 5:2
[8] 1 Timothy 1:12-16
[9] Anonymous
[10] Philippians 1:29
[11] 1 John 5:12
[12] This poem was written by E.H. Hamilton,
     After hearung of the death of his missionary
     colleague Jack Vinson. Vinson was martyred
     In 1931 and showed no fear of death to his
     Chinese captors, telling them,
     "Kill me if you wish. I will go straight to God."
[13] Deuteronomy 33:25
[14] Mark 8:35
[15] John 12:24

Chapter 2

Endure Hardness as a Good Soldier

2 And the things that thou hast heard of me among many witnesses, the same commit thou to faithful men, who shall be able to teach others also.

Sometimes the most obvious details escape the most diligent observer. This is especially true when we begin to analyze the things that make what we do effective. The teacher may think it is the material; the actor may think it is the script. The preacher may think it is the content of his sermon, and the disciple-maker may scrutinize his program. The fact is, though, that it is the person himself that is the most important factor.

For this reason, Paul emphasized "faithful" men: that is where Timothy was to invest his time and effort. Although he must be compassionate to the spiritually weak, and minister to their needs, it is the faithful who will be productive and need to be developed. They will be able to teach others also and will bring forth fruit after their own kind. It is counterproductive to spend all of our time trying to make men of unfaithful character productive, while neglecting the building up of healthy saints.

It matters who is doing the teaching or the preaching. It is the character of the messenger that gives credence to the message. Had

Jesus not lived the life that He did, would the words that He spoke have had the same impact? Jesus not only spoke the truth, He *is* the truth. Therefore what He says and what He does are the same. His life is a demonstration of His words. If it were otherwise, it would be discernable that either His words are false or His life is. Truth is without contradiction.

Character is everything. Faithful men are those who endeavor to consistently walk in truth. By God's grace they practice what they preach and they can be trusted to apply what God teaches them. Even though they are fallible, their obvious purpose is to do the will of God. When they fail, they are quick to repent. When they fall, they quickly stand up again. They can be trusted to do what is right and their word is their bond.

Paul knew this. He exemplified faithfulness. He constantly held up his example as the guideline for disciples coming after him. Timothy—or we—may well ask Paul, "What shall I pass on to those whom I teach?"

And he would answer, "*The things that thou hast heard of me among many witnesses.*"

Because of the little preposition "of," we might ponder, did he mean the things we have heard about him, or the things we have heard from him?

He meant both. Paul was not reluctant to point to his own example. This was not pride, but confidence born of the fact that he purposed that his life should manifest Christ. He could conscientiously state, "*And herein do I exercise myself, to have always a conscience void of offence toward God, and toward men.*" [1]

To the Corinthian believers he said,

"*Be ye followers of me, even as I also am of Christ. Now I praise you, brethren, that ye remember me in all things, and keep the ordinances as I delivered them to you.*" [2]

This verse indicates we are to embrace what we have heard about him (his reputation) i.e., follow me even as I follow Christ; and what we have heard from him (his doctrine) i.e., keep the ordinances as

32

delivered them to you.

Nor was Paul slow to exhort young men to have his same purpose; to be an exemplar. In a previous letter to Timothy he had urged, *"Let no man despise thy youth; but be thou an example of the believers, in word* [that is, everything that comes out of your mouth], *in conversation* [that is your deportment, your lifestyle, what you convey by the things you do and embrace], *in charity, in spirit, in faith, in purity."* [3] The man is the key. We bring forth fruit after our own kind. As the old English proverb says, "You can't make a silk purse out of a sow's ear."

God-given Method

Not only Paul's Gospel was given him by revelation, but also the means of propagating it. Paul had not been on the mountain listening as Jesus gave the great commission to the eleven disciples that witnessed his ascension, but it is apparent that he got the message—and took it to heart—he "heard" it, and he obeyed it. Paul employed the method that Jesus had instituted. Although Jesus had preached to the multitudes, and literally thousands of people had heard his message, his concentration was on teaching a handful of faithful men. To them he revealed the Father's character and the secrets of the kingdom. He taught them, corrected them, coached them and commissioned them. And what was that commission?

> *"Go ye therefore, and teach all nations, baptizing them in the name of the Father and of the Son and of the Holy Ghost; teaching them to observe all things whatsoever I have commanded you."* [4]

And he added a promise,

"And lo I am with you always even unto the end of the world." [5] Obviously this commission extended beyond that generation.

The teaching of the nations would be accomplished by making disciples within those nations who would multiply like benevolent bacteria. You can't teach nations, you can teach people. You don't baptize nations; you baptize people. It is individuals who commit to observing to do whatsoever Jesus commanded. The commission is "Make Disciples."

The pace Paul set could accomplish the work that was committed to the church. Otherwise he would not have insisted that Timothy follow his example and pass it on to other generations. This pattern should continue until the end of the world. His total dedication was to carry the Gospel to every nation, *warning every man and teaching every man in all wisdom that he might present every man perfect in Christ Jesus.*[6] This is how the church is built—living stones laid together.

An Everlasting Principle

An ideal embraces a principle that works to move things toward a specific goal. In order to fulfill the commission that Jesus entrusted to the church—that of teaching all nations and preaching the Gospel to every creature—two options are before us: add to the numbers, or multiply them. Jesus' command implied multiplication, and Paul's instruction to Timothy confirmed it.

Consider these numbers, this is the ideal. If the day he received Paul's letter Timothy began to reach one thousand souls a day with the Gospel, and his lifespan should be extended indefinitely, if there had been no increase in the earth's population from the perhaps two billion of Paul's day, Timothy would still have about four thousand years of work to do.

If, on the other hand, he had won and discipled one person each year that in turn had done the same, after thirty-one years—if each convert had ideally replicated the scenario—the number would have multiplied to 2,147,483,648; well over the two billion mark.

Confusion prevails today between two things that are quite different, "life in Christ" and "the Christian Religion." Religion, as that word is used today, is part of the natural world system, and perceives the church to be an organization. Its goals therefore are organizational and its methods commensurate with that view. There is a dependency on "professional" leadership both at home and on foreign fields. Because the traditional view of "church" is institutional, and the "commission" a means of advancing that institution, the train-ing of qualified men is largely academic. That is not consistent with the biblical view, which is simple, practical, spiritually motivated and, above all, effective. According to this word, the ministry of the servant of the Lord is first of all to hear, and then to commit what is heard unto faithful men who in turn will teach others.

Hearing means more than recognizing audible sounds. It means paying attention and obeying the message; replicating the pace that has been set for us. In other words, what is needed today is not pro-fessional "leadership" but simple discipleship. In the church, lead-ing men aright and equipping them for the work is the result of fol-lowing Christ. True discipleship is the parent of true leadership; first we follow, then we lead.

Paul set an example of evangelism, Spirit-filled living and holi-ness. He had a conscience void of offense toward God and toward men. He set a pace of following the Holy Spirit in spite of the fact that this would cause him to stand alone, contrary to the whole soci-ety and sometimes even his Christian brethren.

He told Timothy, "The things that thou hast heard of me among many witnesses, the same commit thou to faithful men, who shall be able to teach others also." The phrase "faithful men" is not limited to educated men, ordained men, especially talented men, or profes-sionals, but men of faithful character who will readily respond to the Word and leadings of the Holy Spirit regardless of the cost. To such men Timothy was to commit the things that he had heard.

He was to teach them with the expectation that they in turn would teach others also. The teaching they received would have imparted to them the vision to pass it on. We are builders in the temple of God.[7] Houses are built of oaks, not acorns; therefore the servant of the Lord not only produces fruit, but also guides that fruit to a mea-sure of maturity. In Proverbs we read that *the fruit of the righteous is a tree of life.*[8] Think on that—"The fruit is a tree."

Our responsibility is immediate obedience to the Word and the leading of the Holy Spirit. It falls on us to teach to others those things to which we ourselves have responded.

Since we are servants of the Lord, this is our ministry, yours and mine. If each member of the body seeks to be a faithful man, there will be no lack of leadership because the local church or assembly will be a constant source of new leaders blossoming from among its ordinary members. Our ministry, then, includes obedience, evangelism, and the teaching of faithful men. This we might call "follow-up" work. Isn't that what Paul's exhortation meant in Colossians 1:28: "[Christ] *Whom we preach, warning every man, and teaching every man in all wisdom, that we may present every man perfect in Christ Jesus?*"

3 *Thou therefore endure hardness, as a good soldier of Jesus Christ.*

Paul was most familiar with the soldier of the Roman army. He literally spent years in their custody. He was arrested by them, imprisoned by them, guarded by them, even chained to them and, at times protected by them. He knew Roman soldiers. Although they now represented the enemy, he admired them for their discipline and their commitment to duty.

The Roman soldier was a man who, in order to be a recruit, had first to show that he had good character and was a true Roman citizen either by natural birth into a Roman family, or by swearing allegiance to the emperor and taking Roman citizenship. Once the soldier had been issued his uniform and weapons, there followed months of rigorous basic training in weapons handling, tactics and hand to hand combat. Unarmed combat techniques were intended for occasions when being separated from his unit in battle, or being set upon while alone, he would be able to stand.

Once thoroughly trained so that all this was second nature to them, Roman soldiers were then prepared for battle. Collectively they learned strategies and tactics to enable them to fight together as a single unit. They were expected to undertake grueling marches across rough and dangerous terrain in severe weather conditions and then fight long and arduous battles against fierce enemy warriors. Marching up to twenty miles a day, they had to carry their own weapons, food, and equipment, so it was important that they were strong and fit and self-reliant. Above all they had to obey all orders at once without question, no matter what the consequences.

Should men who serve the Lord Jesus Christ be of lesser character? Do these qualities not have a spiritual counterpart in the Lord's servants?

He Endures Hardness

In the world, the good life is the desired goal. The more creature comforts, the better. For those who belong to the world, that's the measure of the good life. It is commonly joked among them, "He that dies with the most toys wins." We know that's not true. Nevertheless, that philosophy appeals to the flesh and has a way of coloring our perspective as well. Their houses get bigger each year, their levels of indebtedness increase with each succeeding generation, their motivation for acquiring education is higher income levels, their homes are converted into entertainment centers, and they buy memberships in high-tech gymnasiums to keep their bodies from deteriorating as a result of the ease of the good life.

Unfortunately, the believers' lifestyle too often reflects that of the society at large. It is no more a matter of "them and us," but of "we." What's important to "them" is important to "us." In a subtle way, this makes what is not important to them not important to us. The goals and priorities of the society around us become those of the believers; and this feels normal because it is that in which we are immersed. Obviously we, the body of Christ, will benefit from the comforts and technological advances of the society in which we exist; but we must be constantly aware of two things: that we cannot serve God and mammon; and that we are in hostile territory behind enemy lines. In other words, although we are in the world, we are not of it. Our goals are different, as is our definition of success.

Much of what the world offers as comfortable and good tends to distract us from that which is eternal and holy. The path of righteousness is, as regards the course of this world, a swim upstream,

37

an uphill course, a path that the present world opposes and rewards with persecution. Paul made that clear to Timothy when he said, *"Yea and all that will live godly in Christ Jesus shall suffer persecution."* [9] The way of truth often presents tough challenges and hard choices. The word "endurance" appears often in scriptures addressing the Christian's life.

Paul, in his analogy, compares Timothy—and us—to a good soldier; a soldier being, by definition, "one who is enlisted in a cause to which he is committed and faithful." His commitment to his enlistment becomes his primary and only duty. It will involve endurance under fire, in trying circumstances and in the face of opposition resolute in its effort to turn him back. One of the traits of a servant of the Lord is his ability and willingness to endure such hardness. This characteristic is carefully avoided by many of God's "soldiers." Is it because we have lost the instinct to do battle against an enemy that has disguised himself as benign? Perhaps we have forgotten the admonition of the apostle Paul:

> *"for unto you it is given in the behalf of Christ not only to believe on him, but also to suffer for his sake."* [10] Jesus Christ himself, *"though he were a Son, yet learned he obedience by the things that he suffered."* [11]

The Hardness of Suffering Need

The church has recently endured a few years of what might be called termite attacks. That is preaching purporting to be true that undermines the integrity of the faith. In the name of "faith," this false preaching has focused the saints on the things the world holds in high esteem, offering them as the reward for believing God's promises. It places emphasis on wealth, comfort, prestige and physical health. None of these, of course, are wrong in themselves if God sees fit to grant them, but if they are an objective—the goal for which we strive to be "spiritual"—they become the antithesis of what the Bible teaches. They are mammon. Nothing is more plainly spoken in the words of the Lord Jesus than, *"You cannot serve God and mammon.*" [12]

If the thought is true that prosperity and health signify the blessing of the Lord, the inverse can easily be concluded; the absence of these is the result of failing Him or being out of His will. But Paul said,

> *"I have learned, in whatsoever state I am, therewith to be content. I know both how to be abased, and I know how to abound: everywhere and in all things I am instructed both to be full and to be hungry, both to abound and to suffer need."* [13]

Paul, at times, lived among wealthy people while he himself was in want. He had no thought that he was less pleasing to the Lord than they, or that he was deprived. He said nothing to them at the time about his present poverty. He later wrote this to them,

> *"And when I was present with you and wanted, I was chargeable to no man: for that which was lacking to me the brethren which came from Macedonia supplied: and in all things I have kept myself from being burdensome unto you, and so will I keep myself."* [14]

The thought of enduring hardness may conjure an idea of intolerable inconvenience, torture, persecution, or exile. Here, though, Paul is addressing a kind of steadfastness that many would not consider necessary. Paul was among the Corinthians without money or resources. They either didn't notice or were unconcerned, yet he did not make his needs known to them. To bear a need in silence in order to maintain a testimony of total dependence on the Lord and not be chargeable to men is a mark of character that honors the Lord. He obviously believed that his service was to the Lord, who was also his provider, and was therefore willing to endure.

When we have a need, it's easy to look to men to meet it. Then we may either beg or hint, hoping that someone will be alert and take pity on us. In so doing we testify that our God is not sufficient and that His promises are not reliable enough for us to trust.

God's promise is that he will supply all of our needs according to His riches in glory by Christ Jesus.[15] Only He knows what our needs are. We are instructed to be content with food and raiment. God's goal is to conform us to the image of His Son, and whatever is required to accomplish that is what we need. If while enduring some period of hardness, we consider ourselves to be deprived or abandoned by God, and begin to appeal to men for relief, or appeal to men in order to accomplish something that God has neither directed nor provided for, we will surely bring reproach.

Consider this: The greatest negative testimony of the Christian community revolves around the raising of money. True or false?

There are millions who would say, "true." This is a sensitive issue.

How would you define poverty? The average American would probably say that poverty is being without enough money to buy the necessities of life. A rich man would be one who has enough money to acquire everything he wants. Riches and poverty, to most of us, would be determined by the lack or abundance of a single commodity, money. Using this standard, we are prone to view the problem of adequate provision from a warped perspective.

In industry and the market place, money is the enabler. It opens new markets and facilitates production and is the measure of profit and loss. It is the bottom line of every transaction. Money is the goal; and the point of every enterprise is the accumulation of money. Even in the world's welfare programs that purport to assist the underprivileged, money is the determinate factor. Almost no one participates without monetary remuneration. It is business. Whenever assistance is proposed, whether it is foreign aid or educational programs, the definition of assistance is "money." When this worldview is superimposed on the activities of the kingdom of God it produces a warped perspective.

We have been trained to see money as the enabler. How many times have we heard variations of this complaint? "God told us to go to Moldavia to evangelize and start a church. However, we can't do it because we don't have enough money." This is not a biblical perspective. God's command contains intrinsically the promise of

God's provision, which may, or may not involve the commodity of money. God chooses. When we need bread, we tend to say we need $2.50 (or whatever the price of bread might be). When we need shoes, we think $80.00 or $40.00, whatever the monetary value is. We tend to see money as the only means to acquire anything. This is the conditioned response of most who have grown up in this world system.

The material promises of New Testament scripture cover every thing we could ever possibly need, but not all that we may want. They do include personal sustenance. Jesus himself promised, "Seek ye first the kingdom of God and his righteousness, and all these things (food and raiment) shall be added unto you." [16] That promise is valid anywhere, at any time, and for any people, but it says nothing about money, as such. While promising us food and raiment and the provision of all that we need, God did not promise us monetary riches. In fact, He warned us about the dangers of such, even going so far as to say,

> "All that [want to be] rich fall into temptation and a snare, and into many foolish and hurtful lusts, which drown men in destruction and perdition." [17]

We can't eat money; we can't wear money. It is worthless for meeting our needs until traded for something that will. God is Lord of heaven and earth. If He should provide the necessary article without the involvement of money, He has saved us a step. Sometimes God does that, and often from surprising sources. He uses money, but the point is that money is not our enabler, God is. And if we are to have a biblical message, and set a biblical example, we must understand that.

The dangers in missing this point are well illustrated on every hand. There are many monuments to man's ability to raise money that have been built in the name of the Lord that do not have God's fingerprints on them. They were some man's idea and he was able to pull it off simply because he had access to sufficient funds. The end result is often a reproach to the Gospel.

41

A few years ago a certain TV evangelist announced that he had had a vision from God to build a multi-storied hospital near the city of Tulsa, Oklahoma. A study by the city indicated that such a hospital was not needed. After insisting that God had commissioned the project, the preacher launched a massive fundraising effort, pressing the viewing public to send the millions of dollars necessary to complete the vision. The last of the funds were sent by a self-professed unbeliever that was willing to help "God" get the job done. After the building was finished, it sat almost vacant for many years before being sold off to a secular organization for another purpose. It became an object of scorn to many detractors of the Gospel.

The real work of God is done *"Not by might, nor by power, but by my Spirit, saith the Lord."* [18] It should be kept in mind that God's provision is promised *"according to God's riches in glory, by Christ Jesus."*

The very first commentary about money when the great missionary movement began is recorded in Acts 3. Peter and John, on their way into the temple to pray, were confronted with a challenge in the form of a forty-year-old genetic cripple. When he begged them for alms, Peter, his pockets figuratively turned inside out, said, *"Silver and gold have I none."* He might have continued, "Sorry, without money there really isn't much that we can do." But he didn't. He said, rather, *"Such as I have give I thee. In the name of Jesus Christ of Nazareth, rise up and walk."* That's how the missionary thrust began; not with silver and gold, but by doing what God alone can do. And that's how it continued and should still continue. It started without any resources except what was provided *"according to God's riches in glory by Christ Jesus."*

Does that mean, then, that God does not use money? Not at all; but when, to the apostle Paul, it seemed appropriate in accomplishing God's purpose, he even refused money, willing to be financially impoverished until God met his need from other sources, that he might prove the faithfulness of God and set a pace for those with whom he labored. Nowhere did he suggest that the work of the Gospel or the ability to carry it out was dependent upon money.

There were many times when Paul labored faithfully on when he had neither money nor anything else

> *"in weariness and painfulness, in watchings often, in hunger and thirst, in fastings often, in cold and nakedness."* [19] He described himself *"as sorrowful, yet always rejoicing; as poor, yet making many rich; as having nothing, yet possessing all things."* [20]

Paul Endured Hardness

While training nationals on the mission field to be missionaries, we taught that the three essentials for proclaiming the Gospel effectively are feet, a mouth and a Bible; plus, of course, the Holy Spirit's enabling. Many, believing that to be true, were enabled to launch works that have had an impact around the world.

I am not suggesting that we never need money in God's work; but it is important for us when tested that we be capable of enduring hardness and deprivation in this area without being discouraged or deterred from what God has called us to do.

This is vital because when we carry the Gospel to nations whose circumstances are far more normal in the scope of world economy than are those of the United States, what do we teach the believers there? What do we offer them that will be their resource in the context of their national poverty? Will we give them access to American funds, or point them to God's promised resources? In order to demonstrate to them God's faithfulness, we must be willing to share their circumstances. We do not need to design for ourselves circumstances that simulate theirs, but at the same time, we must not insure ourselves against experiencing what the people to whom we minister experience every day. That is not consistent with Jesus' example or that of the apostles.

Consider this scenario. Our missionary approaches the field armed with a solid Gospel message and a life of commitment to God. His diligent preaching and godly living bear fruit. Men and women, who have no material wealth, are saved through his ministry. According to the missionary's message, if they seek first the kingdom of God and his righteousness, they can trust God to provide their needs. So they watch this man of God to see what God's resources really are for him. After all, he has been their example in doctrine, in holiness and in lifestyle. He will surely be a dependable example in the matter of trusting God for provision. They notice, however, that whenever his circumstances begin to degenerate to a point nearing theirs, he writes home or calls home, or, in some cases, even goes home.

The message is clear—home is his resource. But they are home. They have no such resource. They have no one to call upon except the Lord. The missionary's job is to teach them, by example, to call upon God who is their faithful resource. He is to demonstrate this by his own life. Otherwise, his only alternative is to put them in touch with his apparent resource, which is America. We are then proclaiming that God cannot accomplish the missionary task through the nationals. His promise is not sufficient in their land.

In the fifties and sixties, my wife and I were missionaries to Korea—at that time a very poor nation. Some of those that attended our missionary training center were extremely poor. One young man in particular had come to us with absolutely nothing and God began to provide him with all that he needed in rather remarkable ways. This young man diligently pursued his responsibilities, and God was faithful to his promise.

One day a young beggar about the same age, obviously in desperate straits, came to the training center gate. It happened that this young missionary trainee answered the knock. As he preached the Gospel to the young beggar, he explained that he himself had only a short time ago been in a similar condition, and even yet had few material possessions, but now he experienced God's daily provision. He told him of God's faithfulness as he had experienced it.

As I watched this, it occurred to me that the only difference between these two was that one of them was seeking first the kingdom of God and His righteousness and the other wasn't. This young missionary and his fellow trainees went on to preach the Gospel without help from America.

Our ministry to them in setting the policy of faith in God as their only resource was enhanced by the fact that we, at the time, were suffering severe lack of financial support and were cast upon the Lord continually for our daily bread. Almost all of our substance came, day by day, by some remarkable local provision.

It is God who determines the circumstances in which we labor, and it is He that determines what we need to accomplish His will. He had allowed us to share the economic level of the people with whom we were working. Provision did not come from America, even though there were those that prayed for us and were concerned about our welfare. Many factors combined to deprive us of finances. As a result, we became dependent upon each other. If the students in the training program received food or money, they shared it with us. What we received we shared with them.

At the same time every day we ate lunch together sitting on the floor around a low table in a little room barely large enough to accommodate our little company. The entrance door was a flimsy sliding frame, the bottom half of which was covered with thin mahogany plywood, and the top with paper. One day we gathered around the table to give thanks despite the fact that there was no food to set upon it. The meal time turned into an extended prayer meeting during which we were blessed and encouraged. Some of the prayers included petition for food.

At the end of the "lunch" time, we rose from prayer and, trying to slide the door open to exit were unable to move it; something heavy was holding the door through which we had all entered only a short time before. One of the young men climbed out of the window, and discovered that our problem was a one hundred kilogram sack of rice, which had been placed there so silently that no one heard the intruder; nor to this day do we know who placed it there. This was only one of many such incidents that God orchestrated to strengthen our faith together.

The extreme hardships that we often felt so sorely proved to be God's perfect provision for the purpose to which He had called us.

45

God was supplying our needs as He saw them. What He withheld enhanced the ministry as much as what He provided.

We don't know what we really need to best accomplish God's purpose. Therefore, our enabler is God and whatever He provides. Lack of money is frequently God's way of preventing us from doing things our way. It is God's option to show deliverance in some other way in order to build faith in those whose circumstances we share; or to apply just the right pressure to our lives to more perfectly conform us to Himself.

Millions of dollars of God's money are raised and spent uselessly, or even detrimentally, every day in our country; and yet in many other places where there is no money at all, God's work goes quietly and efficiently onward. A lack of obedient faith and unwillingness to forsake all is a greater problem than a lack of money. As God's servants, or potential missionaries, we must be more concerned with the caliber of our faith in God's promises, and our willingness to suffer, than about the provision we think will be adequate.

> *"When I sent you out without purse or scrip,"* Jesus asked His disciples, *"lacked ye anything?"*

> *"Nothing, Lord,"* was their reply. [21]

Enduring Danger and Persecutions

In 2 Corinthians 11:23-26 Paul speaks of a kind of hardness that comes more readily to mind when we think of endurance. Jesus called upon his disciples to forsake all—for what? Ultimately for eternal glory and kingdom rewards; but in the immediate future, for persecution, the loss of all things, suffering and imprisonment. Paul's labors brought him into such circumstances.

> *"...In stripes above measure, in prisons more frequent, in deaths oft. Of the Jews five times received I forty stripes save one. Thrice was I beaten with rods, once was I stoned. Thrice I suffered shipwreck, a night and a day I have been in the deep; in journeyings often, in perils of waters, in perils of robbers, in perils by mine own countrymen, in perils*

46

by the heathen, in perils in the city, in perils in the wilderness, in perils in the sea, in perils among false brethren."

Some of these things we may experience once or on an infrequent basis. A shipwreck or a frightening situation that happened once we may report as an adventure. But beaten with rods, stoned, tortured nearly to death, in prison over and over again because of persistent preaching? How long would we be willing to endure that before finding something else to do? These were continuing things with Paul. He had a calling and a job to do, and he intended to continue until it was done. These things were designed to make him quit, but his purpose was to be a faithful man.

We may endure similar things, and even rejoice in them for a while, but when the pressures of enduring persecution and physical pain continue, there may come a willingness to forfeit that which causes the pain. Paul's exhortation is, Endure! *"Endure hardness as good soldiers."* And he backed this up by his own example.

To follow Paul's example requires a calling from God and a conviction that we are in the center of his will. It is almost a certainty that our commitment to obey God will be tested. Something will challenge our confidence that we had the mind of the Lord when we chose the path that led us to this trying circumstance.

Enduring Privation and Physical Discomfort

In 2 Corinthians 11: 27 Paul, in his litany of things he endured, includes, *"Weariness and painfulness, in watchings often, in hunger and thirst, in fastings often, in cold and nakedness."* Over the years we have had opportunity to observe many prospective missionaries: hard workers who have manifested humility when rebuked, corrected or exhorted, and even retained their joy when facing reprimand. In some cases, however, no matter how tough an exterior, how thick a skin an individual may have, there is a weak spot. During days of isolation and lack of provision, when there's no fire in the stove to take the chill off for days at a time, or when there is no food to set on the table through a few consecutive mealtimes, joy begins to evaporate, scowls replace cheerfulness, and carnal complaining spirituality.

These are tests. God has promised that He will never leave us nor forsake us.[22] He is in our trouble with us.[23] The God that promised to supply our needs cannot lie.[24] Two outstanding incidents in my life taught me this truth.

The first was in Eugene, Oregon where, while still very young in the Lord, I had gone to start a rescue mission. God had impressed me with two scripture verses.

The first: *"Seek ye first the kingdom of God and his righteousness and all these things* [food and raiment] *shall be added unto you."* [25]

And the other: *"Be careful for nothing; but in everything by prayer and supplication with thanksgiving let your requests be made known unto God."* [26]

As a young believer I had concluded from these words that God is my provider, to whom alone I was to make my needs known. So that became our policy.

We overcame obstacles and navigated several crises with God's provision. The second winter—an extremely cold one—our furnace oil tank ran dry and there was no money available to fill it. The old, poorly insulated building we occupied became cold and remained increasingly so for several days. Though we were normally upbeat and cheerful, as the cold persisted our countenances changed, and by murmuring and griping, each of us added to the misery of the rest. Prayer became difficult and complaining easy.

Why was God not supplying heat? After much complaining to God and agonizing over our discomfort, I began to realize the carnal attitude we had developed and became impressed that he was providing what we really needed; not oil, but circumstances to reveal the condition of our hearts. The solution was true repentance from our carnal reaction to circumstances and confession of our sin of unbelief. When we prayed again, acknowledging our fault and petitioning God—not for oil—but for right hearts, God answered by first changing our attitudes in our circumstance, and then he provided heat.

The second was in Pohang, South Korea where, in 1959, my family and I had gone to be missionaries. Our policy had not changed. The Lord himself was still our sole supplier. Korean winters were severe, and the houses were not insulated. Without money for fuel or food, we depended on God's miraculous provision from day to day. It was exciting to see his daily solutions. During our first winter we were without transportation, heat and, from time to time, food. Our paper windows and doors provided no protection against the sub-zero temperatures. The long walks to the outlying villages to preach and distribute tracts were exhausting, but bearable. The sometimes meager meals that followed were adequate. The constant cold, however, was debilitating. When you are tired, hungry and cold over an extended period of time, discouragement can predictably result. My wife did not complain, and my children, who were at that time twenty months and three-years-old, seemed to fare well; but my faith wavered.

"I am not man enough to be a missionary," I told God, "Please send us home."

If God answered that prayer, the answer was "No."

We endured that winter, and now we look back on what was a glorious beginning to several fruitful years that even now continue to bear fruit. What a disaster it would have been if God had given me what I asked. No, he gave us what we needed.

During that lowest and hardest time of my life, as I lay on the floor of our Korean hut reading 2 Timothy 2, I realized, "This is Paul's missionary training course. **Timothy is not to be simply a theologian, he is to be a soldier**. God, that's what you're teaching me. This is what I need. This is what I have heard of Paul that I am to teach faithful men that they may be able to teach others also. Thank you, Lord."

Called to the work, a servant of the Lord will not normally enjoy a protected environment away from harsh trials or the trouble and vituperation of some who oppose the Gospel. He will need to be one of God's "tough guys." He needs the hide of a rhinoceros to withstand hard circumstances and perhaps the barbs of critics; and the heart of a dove to have compassion for the lost. It doesn't hurt to have a sense of humor as well so that he can see the light side of sometimes hard situations.

The hardness almost caused me to consider forsaking the call of God. But through it I learned that God is faithful: He never tests us beyond our endurance.[27] His trials are to perfect us, not destroy us. When your tests come, know that God has not forsaken you. He has planned for your provision and your escape, and in the end—no matter what the end might be—is victory. Paul had learned to endure even this hardness. The path is well trodden, and the pace has been set for you. You are not the first to walk this way, nor are you alone.

Bear in mind that the enemy of your soul, now that you are saved and have committed to serve the Lord, seeks to frustrate your service. We learn from the Old Testament that Satan's lofty place in the heavenlies before his fall was one of perfection and wisdom. When he was cast down to the earth, he knew how to instigate rebellion against God. He is no less wise today. In fact, Jesus said, "The children of this world are in their generation wiser than the children of light." [28] Through subtle means Satan tries to derail God's children.

In the wilderness, Jesus experienced Satan's doubt-provoking strategy. Desperately hungry from forty days of fasting, he stood face to face with the adversary listening to his challenge, "If thou be the Son of God, turn these stones into bread." In other words, "You're hungry. God is letting you starve. Do for yourself what God has not done for you. Feed your flesh." Jesus would not satisfy his flesh by doing what the Father had not initiated, especially at Satan's instigation.

God had not forsaken Jesus. This was a battle that had to be won. Jesus was tempted in the lust of the flesh, and then in the lust of the eyes and in the pride of life before this confrontation ended.[29] He was tempted in every way we are tempted; yet without sin. [30]

Many temptations designed to stumble God's faithful men come in times of physical privation, oppressive weariness or great discomfort to the flesh, when their body is exhausted, their mind is weary and their will is weak. Saints who are governed by their feelings are especially vulnerable to such attacks. In such circumstances many succumb to the devastating blows of the adversary because they have been ignorant or unheeding of the command to endure hardness as good soldiers. They were not prepared for the test: they didn't see it coming in spite of the many warnings in the Bible. Hardness, then, includes, but is not limited to, hunger, thirst, cold, nakedness and physical exhaustion. This should not come as a surprise to Bible-reading Christians because they understand that we are at war, unless they have believed another Gospel.

Enduring Without Self-pity

There is yet another dimension to enduring hardness. Two obvious dangers that the scriptures warn about and emphasize strongly are sex and money. In ignoring these biblical cautions, men who have ascended sometimes to dizzying heights of fame as evangelists, pastors or healers have stumbled and brought great reproach on the Gospel. There is a third danger that, although not as obvious, can also be catastrophic: self-pity.

Self-pity leads to self-preservation, often taking us out of the battle at the time our self-sacrifice would have had the greatest impact in the fight. Self-pity causes us to condone—even encourage—others forsaking their responsibilities and being distracted from their duties in order to pamper us and cater to our desire to be consoled.

In war, it is more to the enemy's advantage to wound our soldiers than to kill them, because other soldiers are distracted from their lethal duties by the need to attend to their wounded comrades. Therefore, those who are able to carry on in spite of their wounds are an asset, while those who are disabled become a liability.

This is true also in spiritual warfare. It is our duty to care for our wounded and our disabled; but if our disability is the result of self-pity because we are unprepared or unwilling to endure hardness, it becomes an unnecessary burden to others.

In Paul's letter to the Philippians he mentions Epaphroditus whom Paul considered a man of noble character. Epaphroditus had been sent from the church at Philippi to work with Paul. His service had been diligent, making him a real asset. Although he had become sick "nigh unto death" he refused to allow it to derail his service to Paul. Now it is time for him to return. Paul writes:

> *"Yet I supposed it necessary to send to you Epaphroditus, my brother and companion in labor, and fellow soldier, but your messenger, and he that ministered to my wants. For he longed after you all, and was full of heaviness, because that ye had heard that he had been sick. For indeed he was sick nigh unto death: but God had mercy on him; and not on him only, but on me also, lest I should have sorrow upon sorrow...because for the work of Christ he was nigh unto death, not regarding his life, to supply your lack of service to me."* [31]

Epaphroditus was a true soldier who endured hardness. He was full of heaviness—not because his lot was hard, or because his sickness was severe—but because his friends at Philippi had heard that he was sick. He was concerned for them, not for himself. Self-pity is contradictory to the concept of enduring hardness. Seeking sympathy is no different than seeking anything else from man instead of from God. The command is the same—endure hardness as a good soldier.

There may be those among us who will judge the preceding remarks as extreme or brand them as heroics. In many places where the battle is more evident, however, there are heads nodding agreement. Read again the Book of Acts. Review the history of the church from that day to the present. Look beyond America at the experience of most of the present day church. These are not extreme views. Even the hardest things are not without purpose in God's arrangement of our lives. Remember God's goal, "To conform us to the image of Christ." Our circumstances are of little importance; our deportment in those circumstances is of utmost importance. Through all of the hard things that Paul endured, he learned some things, and he passed them on to us; but he could not make us learn them. He could only make us aware of how they are learned.

"I have learned," he said, *"In whatsoever state I am, therewith to be content. I know both how to be abased, and I know how to abound: everywhere and in all things I am instructed both to be full and to be hungry, both to abound and to suffer need. I can do all things through Christ which strengtheneth me."* [32]

Contentedness, a quiet spirit and a peaceful demeanor in difficult times, was something Paul had to learn. He developed these through the experience of suffering. This conviction had settled firmly and quietly upon Paul's consciousness:

"All things work together for good to them that love God, to them who are the called according to his purpose."

That is what he wrote in Romans 8:28. Many folks quote that verse. Some even stop quoting after "All things work together for good." But we must read on to verse 29, "For whom he did foreknow, he also did predestinate to be conformed to the image of his Son, that he might be the firstborn among many brethren."

As Paul demonstrated, we who trust the Lord with our lives need not avoid God's hard places. We know, as Paul did, that all things are working together to conform us to the image of the Lord Jesus.[33] That's God's stated purpose; is it not also our desire?

(Endnotes)

[1] Acts 24:16
[2] 1 Corinthians 11:1,2
[3] 1 Timothy 4:12
[4] Matthew 28:19
[5] Matthew 28:20
[6] Colossians 1:28
[7] Ephesians 2:21,22; 4:16; 1 Corinthians 3:9,10
[8] Proverbs 11:30
[9] 2 Timothy 3:12
[10] Philippians 1:29
[11] Hebrews 5:8
[12] Matthew 6:24
[13] Philippians 4:11,12
[14] 2 Corinthians 11:9
[15] Philippians 4:19
[16] Matthew 6:33
[17] 1 Timothy 6:9
[18] Zechariah 4:6
[19] 2 Corinthians 11:27
[20] 2 Corinthians 6:10
[21] Luke 22:35
[22] Hebrews 13:5
[23] Psalm 46:1
[24] Titus 1:2
[25] Matthew 6:33
[26] Philippians 4:6

Chapter 3

Unentangled

4 No man that warreth entangleth himself with the affairs of this life; that he may please him who hath chosen him to be a soldier. 5 And if a man also strive for masteries, yet is he not crowned, except he strive lawfully. 6 The husbandman that laboreth must be first partaker of the fruits. 7 Consider what I say; and the Lord give thee understanding in all things

Paul seems much taken with the analogy of war and soldiering. No doubt because of the time in which he was living, the circumstances he was enduring, and the prospect of the death he would soon be dying. Rome was waging all-out war upon the Christians who were facing real military forces before their capture and hungry lions afterward. Many had bravely faced their captors, while others had fled, gone underground or defected. This was war. Paul, as much as he was able at this point, was training soldiers in a real conflict.

That war has never ended; it has heated and cooled, or changed appearance over the centuries, but the fact is, the saints of today are facing the same adversary in the same conflict with the same consequences as then, for both the victors and the vanquished. When we read Paul's words today, they seem romanticized and a little make-

55

believe. But you may be sure that's not how they seemed to Timothy. And if we, even in our distracted, fun-loving generation should see the present world through the eyes of the Holy Spirit, we would see that the analogy still fits. The war, though more subtle, is still as heated and deadly as ever.

There will soon come a day all over the world that the war will once again break out in the form that Paul's generation experienced it. Even in our peaceful nation, it is rumbling below the surface like a volcano ready to explode. In other places in the world the magma has already erupted and the lava of persecution is flowing.

The faithful men in Paul's earlier reference are men who, as Paul expects Timothy to do, have taken the warfare seriously. In so doing, their purpose will be to please Him who has chosen them to be soldiers. This Christian walk is not a game. It is not a haphazard or half-hearted practice of whatever amount of religion fits my schedule or suits my agenda, but a battle in which the forces of the adversary have pledge themselves to the destruction of God's plan and the frustration of His purpose. We are the frontline. How does that line look from where you are?

If you answered that the way I suspect you did, you're right, we don't look that good. But God has chosen the weak things of this world to confound the mighty, and it is God's servants, members of His body, that have been chosen warriors in this eternally influential struggle. God will show His victory, and manifest His glory through the church to the principalities and powers that seek to overthrow His dominion.

It would appear that, to some professing believers, this war is quite incidental to the satisfying of individual whims. Some appear to be deeply engrossed in things that carry no eternal weight whatsoever, while the command of God is, for the present, unheeded. Obedience that is not immediate is, in the immediate, disobedience. It is therefore imperative that the servant of the Lord be without entanglement in order that he might be available to quickly respond to the call of God and the direction of His Spirit. In a moment we are going to see what that means.

Perhaps there are among the readers of Timothy's letter those who are not familiar enough with war to be impressed with the challenge of it. For them, games rule the day and occupy the mind. In twenty-first century America, some of the most monetarily successful people are professional athletes. They strive for masteries: Soccer's World Cup, Hockey's Stanley Cup, Olympic medals, Super Bowl rings; these, among other trophies for other sports, to them are the most prized awards worth almost anything to gain. But notice how few attain them. Those who do are dedicated, sacrificial, hardworking, single-minded and play by the rules. It costs something to win—more than most people are willing to pay. But this is Paul's exhortation to Timothy and to all of us who follow, "Run that ye may obtain." [1] This is how faithful men live the Christian life.

What we sow we reap. The character we demonstrate is the character we produce in those we mentor. What we are is what our disciples will become. Every tree brings forth fruit after its own kind. We must first be partakers of what we seek to share with others.

The word "unentangled" is not a synonym for "disconnected," nor does it mean irresponsible or unengaged. Every person has societal obligations. If he has a family, he is responsible for their welfare. Everyone is obligated to pay rent, to buy groceries, to pay taxes and to fulfill other requirements that constitute "the affairs of this life." This is true whether he is a servant of the Lord or not. In Paul's exhortation there is no advocacy for a monastic lifestyle. Paul demonstrated complete unentanglement from the affairs of this life while working with his hands to feed himself and those who ministered with him.[2] Let's consider what it means, then, to be unentangled.

Often around military installations there is a barbed wire barrier. This "concertina wire" has to be handled by the men who install it. Handling it discreetly, they will not become entangled in it. There is a difference between handling and being entangled. So it is with the affairs of this life. Apart from God's oversight, they can, like the barbed wire, become entanglements hindering our service to God. But if we are single-minded and led by the Spirit of God, we will fulfill all the responsibilities that comprise the affairs of this life without being entangled or distracted from fighting the war or running the race or being first partakers of the fruit as God's husbandmen.

In Jeremiah 35:7 we read of the Rechabite family in Israel. They were told by their father, "*Ye shall drink no wine, neither ye, nor your sons forever. Neither shall ye build house, nor sow seed, nor plant vineyard, nor have any: but all your days ye shall dwell in tents; that ye may live many days in the land where you be strangers.*" These were strangers in the land; their permanent treasures were not there. But they could live there long and successfully if they did not set their hearts upon personal possessions, wealth and acquisition of things. Israel was not their permanent home.

This among all the other things in the Old Testament was written for our admonition. It describes our relationship to this present world, in which we are to live as pilgrims. This is not where our inheritance is. As long as we do not become enamored of the things that tempt us to live like those whose roots are here, we will remain unentangled and able to please Him who has called us to be soldiers.

Throughout history, the masses of the earth's population, occupied with temporal existence, have formed a faceless background against which a few heroes of faith have stood out, writing on the pages of history the message of eternal inheritance. Some of them, famous for their accomplishments, died as heroes; some as martyrs. Not all were men or women of extraordinary gifting. Most were not famous in the world's terms or, in some cases, even known. Many of them lived and died in obscurity. But they all had one thing in common—the only thing that mattered—they were faithful to the Word; their sights were firmly set on things above where Christ sits on the right hand of God.

"*These all died in faith, not having received the promises, but having seen them afar off, and were persuaded of them, and embraced them, and confessed that they were strangers and pilgrims on the earth. For they that say such things declare plainly that they seek a country. And tru-*

ly, if they had been mindful of that country from whence they came out, they might have had opportunity to have returned. But now they desire a better country, that is, an heavenly: wherefore God is not ashamed to be called their God: for he hath prepared for them a city." [3]

There are many things that pertain to our daily lives that are normal, ordinary and even necessary, which can become major entanglements if we set our hearts upon them. We have the warning in scripture, *"If riches increase, set not your heart upon them."* [4] The problem of entanglement is not with what is in our hand, but what is in our heart.

Entangled by Things

Two things that we hold extremely dear in our free society are our right to personal freedom, and our right to gain wealth. Beware of "things" and "rights." The right of ownership, the right to do as I please, or not to do as I please—these are important things to us. We can point to history and proudly say, "Much blood was shed to acquire these rights. They were bought and paid for, and they are mine." That is well and good, but there is another issue here, one that supersedes all that my earthly citizenship affords me. It is the cross.

The apostle Paul wrote, *"He that is called in the Lord, being a servant, is the Lord's freeman: likewise also he that is called, being free, is Christ's servant."* [5]

A simple definition of the cross, which we are commanded to take up daily, is, *"Not my will, but thine be done."* [6] If we are servants of the Lord, our rights are always subordinate to what God's will is in the present circumstance. Sometimes, like the saints described in the book of Hebrews, we must take joyfully the spoiling of our goods.

In John 12:25, Jesus said, *"He that loveth his life shall lose it; and he that hateth his life in this world shall keep it unto life eternal."*

This implies that there are riches that far exceed the value of anything we might lose in this life through letting go of the "good things." They were ballast weighing us down and making us less agile in the spiritual battles into which we were thrust. Many men have lost their effectiveness through holding too tightly or pursuing too hotly what were for other men legitimate rewards, but had nothing to do with the course God had set them on. It is dangerous for us to so earnestly desire what can become distractions and entanglements to us, whether they be rights or material things.

Paul, pace-setter for Timothy and you and me, said,

> *"But what things were gain to me, those I counted loss for Christ. Yea doubtless, and I count all things but loss for the excellency of the knowledge of Christ Jesus my Lord: for whom I have suffered the loss of all things, and do count them but dung, that I may win Christ."* [7]

It seems Paul is saying that when one suffers loss in the pursuit of God's perfect will, whether it be great or small, or even painful, he is indeed entangled if he would consider changing course to gain it back. Beware, beloved, of holding anything too dearly.

A.W. Tozer, in his book The Pursuit of God, writes:

> *Before the Lord God made man upon the earth, he first prepared for him by making a world of useful and pleasant things for his sustenance and delight. In the Genesis account of the creation, these are called simply "things." They were made for man's uses, but they were meant always to be external to the man and subservient to him. In the deep heart of man was a shrine where none but God was worthy to come. Within him was God; without a thousand gifts which God had showered upon him.*
>
> *Our woes began when God was forced out of his central shrine and "things" were allowed to enter. Within the human heart, "things" have taken over. Men have now, by nature, no peace within their hearts, for God is crowned there no longer, but there in the moral dusk stubborn and*

aggressive usurpers fight among themselves for first place on the throne.

Our Lord referred to this tyranny of "things" when he said to his disciples: "if any man will come after me, let him deny himself, and take up his cross, and follow me. For whosoever will save his life shall lose it, and whosoever will lose his life for my sake shall save it."

Romantic Entanglement

Timothy was a young man. Paul was an old man, but he had once been a young man. He understood youth and the hormones that race through the bodies of young men. That's why, a little later in this letter he tells Timothy to "flee youthful lusts." Is it possible that men as godly as Paul or Timothy experienced those feelings and struggled with hormonal distractions? Of course they did! The prime instinct of the man that God created was to reproduce. Sex is not sin. The first instruction given to Adam was *"multiply, fill the earth."* How could that have been possible without sex? And why would it have ever happened if God had not instilled in man the desire to pursue it? God's word says, *"The marriage bed is undefiled. But…"* [8]

Since we know that "but" is a transitional word with power to reverse everything, we realize that there is a problem connected to this originally God-given desire. The problem is the human nature that has perverted what God has given. It is to be under the control of the Spirit, reserved for marriage. Until marriage it is a means of developing maturity, self-discipline, patience and temperance. In God's time and according to God's purpose and provision he arranges marriage, and sexual relations become a wonderful part of that relationship.

What Paul calls youthful lusts are to be managed, kept under control, otherwise they become distractions or entanglements. I recall, as a young man many years ago, being at a Navigators conference at Colorado Springs. I was assigned to a dormitory room with another young man from California who was still in military service and spending his leave at the conference. The Glen Ayre Campus seemed to be populated by an extraordinary number of attractive young ladies, by whom our young soldier seemed to be almost continually distracted. One day, as he stood looking out the window he made a comment about one of the young ladies that could be seen walking across the lawn.

I reproved him gently for what I considered his preoccupation with the women. His response was, "If I'm not looking, how will I find a wife?"

"Do you think God wants you to be married?" I asked.

"Yes, he does." He replied.

"Then don't you think he is concerned enough to arrange it in His way in His time?"

He was not convinced of that, therefore he spent his time distracted from some wonderfully edifying ministry which God had obviously sent him to absorb. Furthermore, because of his state of mind, his presence added nothing to the edification of those who shared his space. He was entangled.

Romantic entanglement is not confined to the young. In our age of exaggerated priority given to sexual aggrandizement and companionship it seems it is considered beyond imagination that anyone, single, divorced or widowed should be celibate. That thinking, so prevalent in the world, has even penetrated the professing church. The affairs of this life include even the "affairs" of this life. Sensuality is so common that the problem is not recognized for what it is until it reaches intensity beyond recall.

There are many potential "soldiers" that have been distracted from fruitful service in the will of God by yielding to normal, but nonetheless sensual desires that have caused them to make choices through which they were irretrievably ensnared in partnerships that have entangled them.

"Art thou bound to a wife?" Paul wrote in 1 Corinthians 7:27, *"Seek not to be loosed. Art thou loosed from a wife? Seek not a wife."*

In the same chapter he continues,

> *"But I would have you without carefulness. He that is unmarried careth for the things that belong to the Lord, how he may please the Lord ...There is difference also between a wife and a virgin. The unmarried woman careth for the things of the Lord, that she may be holy both in body and in spirit; but she that is married careth for the things of the world, how she may please her husband."*

Paul considered the married state a gift, and also the unmarried state. He said, *"Every man hath his proper gift of God, one after this manner and another after that."* [9] As long as a man or a woman continues single, it should be considered a gift. We are not to grumble or rebel at it, we are to take advantage of it and serve God with all the liberty that the single state affords. On the other hand, when we are married, we are partakers of a different gift that affords different benefits and produces different results.

If it is obvious from scripture that marriage is of God—and it is evident that most people marry—it is clearly a mistake to allow this to be the one area that is controlled by our lust rather than by our prayer. God's word says,

> *"This is the confidence that we have in him, that, if we ask anything according to his will he heareth us: and if we know that he hear us, whatsoever we ask, we know that we have the petitions that we desire of him."* [10]

If you are single, it is a gift from God. Thank God for it and honor his choice. If you are single, but believe God would have you married, pray according to his will and trust him for it. Get on with seeking first the kingdom of God and his righteousness.

There used to be a sign in the pilots' room at the Bend, OR airport that read, "It's better to be down here wishing you were up there, than to be up there wishing you were down here." Just a little warning about being so anxious to get airborne that you disregard the weather warnings and become entangled by weather in which you should not have been flying. Well, maybe there should be some place to post a sign to warn the restless singles, reading, "It's better to be single wishing you were married, than to be married wishing you were single." Wait on the Lord. Anxiety about marriage, preoccupation with the company of the opposite sex, dating and the pursuit of that which entertains, titillates or satisfies the flesh, are all distractions that can become entanglements with the affairs of this life. God is in charge.

Religious Entanglement

Sometimes we are surprised at how subtle the adversary is. There he is, right within our ranks, wearing our uniform, with our weapon in his hands, and using our training manual to disqualify our soldiers. Everyone can be taught to keep the rules. If he has a religious spirit, he will even be inclined to meticulously conform to law, thinking, erroneously, that he will be thereby counted righteous. External conformity, even to the law, can never produce righteousness; it simply produces Phariseeism.

That was the Apostle Paul's problem before he was saved. By his own testimony, as we read in chapter one, he had served the Lord from his forefathers with a pure conscience. In another place he wrote that concerning the law he had been blameless; but he persecuted the church and killed the saints. As diligently as he kept the rules, it had no bearing on the conversion of his heart. The law can only deal with externals. Only the Spirit of God can perform the washing that regenerates the nature.

Regulating the behavior by the imposition of law cannot change the heart, but a change of heart by the Spirit will regulate the behavior. Sometimes an observing third party may not recognize the difference in the similarly appearing result of these two scenarios, because man looks on the outward appearance and sees only the behavior, but God looks on the heart. What changes the heart is not the law, which is the old covenant; but the Gospel, which is the New Testament.

> *"[He] also hath made us able ministers of the New Testament; not of the letter, but of the spirit; for the letter killeth, but the spirit giveth life."* [11]

The first was that to which man was required to conform; the second was that which Christ did to transform the man and make of him a new creature. New Testament behavior is not accomplished by imposing rules and regulations, but by obedience to the leading of the Holy Spirit.

> *"As many as are led by the Spirit of God, they are the sons of God."* [12]

Paul ministered the New Testament truth to the people of Galatia, and they received it. Several churches were born. Then in Paul's absence Jewish teachers descended upon those churches and taught them that righteousness came through keeping the law. They became intellectually confused because of the carnal logic involved with law-keeping. Doesn't it seem logical that stringent rule-keeping and fervent religiosity adds to the appearance of holiness? Why would God not be impressed with our sacrifice, service and ceremony? All of the things we are being taught are recorded there in the Old Testament scriptures.

> Paul's response was, *"Christ is become of no effect unto you, whosoever of you are justified by the law; ye are fallen from grace."* [13]

There are those who would design laws and regulations from scriptures found in the New Testament books as well, and endeavor to make the saints conform to a code that will make them more "spiritual." Again, conformity to Christ is not accomplished by rules, but rather by obedience to the Spirit on the part of those who hear His voice in the word of God, and see His example in the lives of obedient saints who preach that word and demonstrate that life.

Paul's instruction to the Galatian believers was,

> *"Stand fast therefore in the liberty wherewith Christ hath made us free, and be not entangled again with the yoke of bondage [legalism]."* [14]

Religion is one of the things that qualifies as the "affairs of this life" with which Timothy was warned by Paul not to be entangled.

We, too, need to be alert and heed the warning.

(Endnotes)
1 1 Corinthians 9:24
2 Acts 20:33-35
3 Hebrews 11:13-16
4 Psalm 62:10
5 1 Corinthians 7:22
6 Luke 22:42
7 Philippians 3:7,8
8 Hebrews 13:4
9 1 Corinthians 7:7
10 1 John 5:14,15
11 2 Corinthians 3:6
12 Romans 8:14
13 Galatians 5:4
14 Galatians 5:1

Chapter 4

Suffering, Resurrection and Reward

> **8 Remember that Jesus Christ of the seed of David was raised from the dead according to my gospel: 9 Wherein I suffer trouble, as an evildoer, even unto bonds, but the word of God is not bound. 10 Therefore I endure all things for the elect's sakes, that they may also obtain the salvation which is in Christ Jesus with eternal glory.**

Paul wrote in a letter to the Romans,

> *"I am not ashamed of the gospel of Christ; for it is the power of God unto salvation to everyone that believeth; to the Jew first, and also to the Greek."* [1]

Disregarding the consequences of preaching that forbidden message, he was determined to proclaim the way of salvation so that all who would receive it could take their place among God's elect as partakers of the eternal glory, which is in Christ Jesus. As a result, the apostle finds himself in a Roman prison enduring whatever "all things" might include. Since he is one of the despised Christians "justly" sentenced for denigrating the national religion of emperor worship, and proclaiming instead another hope and a greater king-

67

dom, we can be reasonably sure it would include at the very least ridicule and humiliation.

Even imprisonment and the impending capital punishment prescribed for Paul cannot make him ashamed of the gospel that has procured eternal life for Jew and Gentile alike. There is no amount of trouble that can curb his determination or make his purpose seem less worthwhile. He has even urged Timothy to follow unashamedly in his steps and preach the same gospel also. In so doing, there is something that he must remember. "*Jesus Christ of the seed of David was raised from the dead according to my gospel.*"

There are two important things included in this reminder: the first being that Jesus was of the seed of David; and the second that he was raised from the dead.

Jesus Christ was the seed of David. This is a declaration of his bona fide humanity. Over and over again in the New Testament gospels Jesus refers to himself as the "Son of Man." He is also referred to as the "Son of God": his deity is not in question, but his own emphasis about his identity was that he is the Son of man.

"*For the Son of man,*" he said, "*is come to seek and to save that which was lost.*" [2]

At another time, making a distinction between his humanity and deity, he said,

"*And whosoever speaketh a word against the Son of man, it shall be forgiven him: but whosoever speaketh against the Holy Ghost, it shall not be forgiven him, neither in this world, neither in the world to come.*" [3]

And in yet another place, "*For as Jonas was three days and three nights in the whale's belly; so shall the Son of man be three days and three nights in the heart of the earth.*" [4]

Jesus was the incarnation of the Word by whom the world was created; *all things were created by him and for him, and without him was not anything made that was made.*[5] The Apostle John tells us that *the Word was made flesh and dwelt among us.*[6] However, God is a Spirit; He is invisible and immortal,[7] which means he is not flesh, he cannot be seen and he cannot die. The Word, to redeem humanity, must become humanity.

God prepared for him a human body.[8] As a human being, contrary to God's case, he had a beginning; there was a specific time of conception. While being in the Spirit eternal, he was also a flesh-and-blood mortal that could die. Many find the concept of humanity and Deity in one person difficult to embrace. To some, therefore, he is a mere man and a prophet or a great teacher, but not God. While to others he is God who, although he appears as a man, is not truly human; he is super-human, and he lived and died as God. In both cases there is an attempt to comprehend an infinite truth with a finite understanding. This is a mystery to us because it is unique. *"Now we see through a glass darkly."* [9] It is difficult to understand that Jesus is one hundred percent God and one hundred percent man.

God cannot die; he is immortal. The Father cannot die; the Word cannot die; the Holy Ghost cannot die; only the humanity of Jesus could die. And die he must in order to purge the sin of Adam's fallen race.[10] The first man, Adam, sinned and incurred death, which passed upon every member of his race. Jesus, as the last (terminal) Adam, died the death for Adam's entire race. [11] By being born of a virgin, he became a member of Adam's race without inheriting Adam's sin; hence he is *"the seed of the woman"* prophesied in Genesis 3:15. But we cannot say that Mary is the mother of God, as some do; she is the mother of the man Jesus the Christ—a mortal being with a date of birth and a time of physical death.

By emphasizing that he is the seed of David, Paul is underscoring the fact of Jesus' humanity. The importance of this fact seems obvious, but Paul recognized that Timothy needed to be reminded lest by his preaching some might misunderstand that Deity died for humanity. But since *by man came death by man came the resurrection from the dead.* [12] It was the last Adam that died for the first Adam's sin.

The death of Jesus, however, is not the good news. There are two parts to the gospel. In his letter to the Romans Paul wrote, "[Jesus our Lord] *was delivered for our offenses, and was raised again for our justification.*" [13] He was delivered up or crucified to pay for our offenses, but our justification—which means to be made righteous as though we had never sinned—came through his resurrection. Being raised from the dead he became the second man. Whereas Adam was the first man, head of the first race that became corrupted through sin and had to be put to death, Jesus, by resurrection, became the second man and the head of an entirely new race, without the scourge of sin or the penalty of death impending.

> *"Now if any man be in Christ he is a new creature, old things are passed away behold all things are become new."* [14]

The sin that we had in Adam is done away in Christ and we are justified—without sin. That is the good news!

Like Timothy, we too have to be reminded that the gospel includes the resurrection. Many gospel tracts address Jesus' death on the cross, but fail to emphasize his resurrection. Preachers oftentimes, in the gospel they preach, emphasize only the death of Christ; but it is his resurrection that guarantees our hope.

11 *It is a faithful saying: for if we be dead with him, we shall also live with him: 12 If we suffer, we shall also reign with him: if we deny him he also will deny us: 13 If we believe not, yet he abideth faithful: he cannot deny himself.*

In his first letter to Timothy, Paul had admonished him to charge those who are rich in this world not to be high-minded nor to trust in their riches which are at best uncertain, but to trust in God because it is he that has given us richly all things to enjoy.[15] Some folks make that sound like everything is given to the believers in order that they may live a life of enjoyment. When they read, *"Being justified freely by his grace through the redemption that is in Christ Jesus,"* [16] they conclude correctly that our redemption is by grace and that it is free then they surmise incorrectly that in following Jesus there will be no cost. After all, how can there be a cost for something that is free? Furthermore, in emphasizing God's goodness and declaring his inescapable love for us Paul wrote,

> *"He that spared not his own Son, but delivered him up for us all, how shall he not with him also freely give us all things?* [17]

Because it is freely given to us does not mean that redemption was without cost. An enormous price was paid. Calvary was the venue of the most priceless sacrifice. Everything that we have received freely was obtained by the Lord Jesus at a great price. Because God has with Christ also freely given us all things, we must not fail to notice that nothing is apart from Him. He paid the price, we share the reward.

Paul, with marvelous consistency taught the same message to everyone. To the Roman church he wrote,

> *"The Spirit itself beareth witness with our spirit, that we are the children of God: and if children, then heirs, heirs of God, and joint heirs with Christ; if so be that we suffer with him, that we may be also glorified together. For I reckon that the sufferings of this present time are not worthy to be compared with the glory that shall be revealed in us."* [18]

So is it inequitable that we should suffer consequences for identifying with our benefactor who gave His all on our behalf? Indeed it is our privilege to be chosen as His soldiers and labor together with God. *It is given to us in the behalf of Christ not only to believe on him, but also to suffer for his sake.* [19] Salvation is free and forever. The consequence of having received that salvation, though, may cost us everything in this life. We who partake in His resurrection partake also in His death; sharing in His reward means also sharing in His suffering. His life, which we have received, was already committed irrevocably to the Father's will.

God did not spring this on us after the fact. His word is filled with the history of those who suffered for His sake. Certainly Jesus didn't keep it a secret. When He called on men to follow Him He had no recruiting posters offering great rewards and huge bonuses. On the contrary, he said,

> *"If any man will come after me, let him deny himself, take up his cross daily and follow me."* [20] He said, furthermore, *"And whosoever doth not bear his cross, and come after me, cannot be my disciple...so likewise, whosoever he be of you that forsaketh not all that he hath, he cannot be my disciple."* [21]

When Timothy received this letter from his imprisoned mentor, he did not know whether Paul was scheduled to be executed by crucifixion, by being impaled on a pole and set afire to light Nero's gardens, or by being fed to hungry lions. But he knew that Paul faced some hideous invention of that blood-thirsty emperor. Even though he proved faithful and courageous, Timothy must have trembled at the prospects; especially because he himself was implicated in Paul's "crimes."

But he could define Paul's source of courage. Paul had just said in the first part of this letter that Christ had abolished death and had brought life and immortality to light through the gospel. Now as Timothy read this exhortation he knew that his mentor was "immortal" because he had already died with Christ. What else could he mean by, *"If we be dead with him we shall also live with him?"*

If Timothy was like the rest of us, suffering was something for which he had no yearning, but should he avoid it if it were the result of faithfulness to his present commitment? No! And here before him in this letter was the encouragement he needed to be steadfast in any event.

"If we suffer with him, we shall also reign with him." What a glorious prospect! What an extravagant reward; suffering is but for a moment, reigning with Him is forever. What's more, it is all "with Him." If we suffer at all, it will be with Him. Has He not said, *"Lo I am with you always,"* [22] and, *"I will never leave you nor forsake you?"* [23] At that very moment Paul must have been resting in the

grace of God to which he had pointed Timothy for strength. All the power of Rome—and all the forces of the Devil who was the power behind Nero's throne—were pressing Paul to deny his Lord, but he trusted in the promise of God that Jude wrote about in his short epistle,

> *"Now unto him that is able to keep you from falling and present you faultless before the presence of his glory with exceeding joy."* [24]

There would be no denying of Christ on Paul's part or on Timothy's either, or on the part of anyone else who has committed the keeping of their soul to him who can keep them from falling. Such denial would be unthinkable—too horrible to contemplate.

But what about the other "denial;" as in self-denial? That means denying myself what I desire to have—withholding. Paul has withheld nothing of himself or of his possessions; all have been fully and finally surrendered to the Lord Jesus, whose he is and whom he serves. His expectation is therefore that there is a crown of righteousness laid up for him. God will withhold nothing! Now, Timothy, it's your turn. And what about us? It's our turn too. Nothing withheld from him, nothing withheld by him. The inverse is also true.

Sometimes, Timothy, circumstances seem to overwhelm our confidence. Our faith fails. But you can be sure that His faithfulness to us will not fail. *"If we believe not yet he abides faithful; he cannot deny himself."*

Perhaps in Timothy's mind's eye there came a vision of Peter, that tough fisherman that had been around boats and water all his life, caught with his companions in a boat far from shore in a storm that terrified even these experienced sailors.[25] Faintly through the gloom they see a "phantom" figure walking on the water. Then they hear him say, *"Be of good cheer; It is I; be not afraid."*

> *And Peter answered him and said, "Lord, if it be thou, bid me come unto thee on the water."*

> *And he said, "Come."*

Peter's faith in Christ gave him courage and impetus to obey, and stepping over the gunwale of that storm-tossed boat he stood upon the water and began to walk to Jesus. No man had done this before. He suddenly realized the magnitude of his circumstance: the waves, the boisterous wind. Fear came, his faith failed and he began to sink. That's when he cried out, "*Lord, save me.*"

> *And immediately Jesus stretched forth his hand, and caught him, and said unto him, "O thou of little faith, wherefore didst thou doubt?"*

Peter, in that wonderful, terrifying moment, although reproved for doubting, found that though he believed not, yet Christ remained faithful; he cannot deny himself. His command stretched Peter to a place beyond his ability to believe; and his faithfulness delivered Peter out of it, even when he doubted. Peter's faith in Christ that had compelled him to obey was no match for the overwhelming circumstances in which he found himself, and which could have destroyed him. But Jesus was there with him in the circumstances. He had not called Peter into a situation in which he himself was not present. He will never do that to any of His disciples. It had been his obedience to Christ that had brought Peter to that situation—clearly over his head. Jesus had known all about that when he bade him come. Peter finished that walk on the water in the arms of the Lord Jesus. It was his faith *in* Christ that launched Peter to do the impossible; but it was the faith *of* Christ that had kept him in the trial and had brought him safely through it.

Paul's words to Timothy carried great authority. His obedience to Christ had brought him to this vile dungeon and the end of his earthly life. Now it was the faith of Christ that was sustaining him in a state of perfect victory.

Paul had understood this when he wrote to the churches in Galatia. Had he not told them,

> *"That a man is not justified by the works of the law but by the faith of Christ, even we have believed in Jesus*

Christ, that we might be justified by the faith of Christ…I
am crucified with Christ: nevertheless I live; yet not I, but
Christ liveth in me: and the life which I now live in the flesh
I live by the faith of the Son of God, who loved me, and
gave himself for me." [26]

It seems that in the Christian life we are "over our heads" much of the time. Faith in Christ brings us into Him and Him into us. From that point on, it is a different life—His life, and the power of it is His faith. God often calls us out, figuratively, onto a limb—and then He saws it off. We are helpless, terrified and unbelieving as we see the limb fall away; but then we are delighted, for there we are, supported, not by the limb, but by the undying faithfulness of our ever-present Lord. Underneath are the everlasting arms. This is His doing. He is teaching us to trust.

14 *Of these things put them in remembrance, charging them before the Lord that they strive not about words to no profit, but to the subverting of the hearers.*

We have choices. Sometimes we forget how many options we have at any given time: options about how to react to circumstances; what to pay attention to, what words to speak, and where to set our affections. We even have the option of whether to defend our words or to submit to one another and allow the truth to prove itself.

Most of us have experienced episodes when saints, in the presence of unbelievers or weak Christians, have argued over doctrines, attacking one another and defending their positions while unwittingly confusing or subverting those who are listening to them contend. Or perhaps we have spent a great deal of time arguing with religious cult members comparing their error with our truth while missing the mark as far as conveying the gospel is concerned. Or maybe you have argued with your spouse over some perceived error concerning an insignificant detail in information he is conveying to a third party, thereby subverting his credibility or yours, and spoiling an opportunity. These constitute striving about words to no profit. The result is that we subvert the hearer.

Although it seems right to defend our rights, it is an obvious misconception that dead men have any rights at all.

"Don't strive about words, Timothy," Paul is instructing. "It isn't profitable." The strife subverts those that listen. The saints are to remember the things about which we spoke earlier; things that are life, and that edify. Arguing about religious doctrines and semantics is academic and tends to be unprofitable, even undermining spirituality. Sound doctrine is preached and taught with certainty, anointing and humility, and translates into faith, obedience and righteousness. Arguments and mindless discussions do not.

(Endnotes)
[1] Romans 1:16
[2] Luke 19:10
[3] Matthew 12:32
[4] Matthew 12:40
[5] John 1:3
[6] John 1:14
[7] 1 Timothy 1:17
[8] Hebrews 10:5
[9] 1 Corinthians 13:12
[10] Hebrews 10:10
[11] 2 Corinthians 5:14
[12] 1 Corinthians 15:21
[13] Romans 4:25
[14] 2 Corinthians 5:17
[15] 1 Timothy 6:17
[16] Romans 3:24
[17] Romans 8:32
[18] Romans 8:16-18
[19] Philippians 1:29
[20] Luke 9:23
[21] Luke 14:27,33
[22] Matthew 28:20
[23] Hebrews 13:5
[24] Jude 24
[25] Matthew 14:22-33
[26] Galatians 2: 16,20

Chapter 5

Rightly Dividing the Word

> **15** *Study to show thyself approved unto God, a workman that needeth not to be ashamed, rightly dividing the word of truth.* **16** *But shun profane and vain babblings; for they will increase unto more ungodliness.* **17** *And their word will eat as doth a canker: of whom is Hymenæus and Philetus;* **18** *Who concerning the truth have erred, saying that the resurrection is passed already; and overthrow the faith of some.*

The servant of the Lord must feed upon the Word of God, diligently absorbing its precepts and learning its language. Hence Paul's command to "Study to show thyself approved…rightly dividing the word of truth." Such diligent pursuit of the scripture must certainly precede any ability to "rightly divide" it. The impossibility to present the word of God simply and understandably, accurately and with the power of the Holy Spirit, without first being a diligent student of it seems obvious.

Today there are many preachers, teachers, evangelists and ministers of various stripe "dividing the word" as they think most fitting. But the effectiveness of any one of these men is determined not by his personality, scholastic achievement or his title, but by whether or not his message is the word of God, delivered fearlessly and with spiritual anointing. How could this be the case if he were not a diligent student of God's word and confident about what it says?

To David, according to Psalm 119, (of which he is presumed to be the author) the word of God was the beginning, the end and the substance of his life and of his career as Israel's king and God's prophet. An extremely busy man, preoccupied with major responsibilities of State, he nevertheless had time to meditate in what he obviously considered the indispensable word of God.

> *"Thy testimonies,"* he wrote, *"have I taken as an heritage forever: for they are the rejoicing of my heart."* [1]
> *"Through thy precepts I get understanding: therefore I hate every false way. Thy word is a lamp unto my feet and a light unto my path."* [2]

No wonder it was indispensable, the everlasting word was his heritage forever, a lamp to keep his feet from stumbling, and a beacon illuminating his path, keeping his goal visible and his direction right. The word of God was the rejoicing of his heart and the source of his understanding. It caused him to recognize error and to hate every false way. With such a testimony as this from such a man as this it seems folly in the extreme for any would-be servant of the Lord to engage the enemy as Paul had, and as Timothy is being encouraged to do without first immersing himself in the word of God. This is done by maintaining a daily, habitual solitary rendezvous with God.

It serves a two-fold purpose: first the simple pleasure of experiencing the quiet, stabilizing atmosphere of the Lord's presence—and the more habitual our engagement becomes, the more palpable his presence seems. David wrote, *"How sweet are thy words to my taste! Yea, sweeter than honey to my mouth!"* [3]

Secondly, it is a purifier. David asks a question and answers it.

> *"Wherewithal shall a young man cleanse his way? By taking heed thereto according to thy word. With my whole*

heart have I sought thee: O let me not wander from thy commandments. Thy word have I hid in my heart, that I might not sin against thee." [4]

It was my privilege while on the mission field, to be acquainted with a fellow missionary who would from time to time stop briefly at our house when his travels took him through our town. When leaving, he would punctuate his stay with a trade mark expression which, like a period at the end of a sentence, would be his parting remark: "Remember," he would say, "purity is power!" And off he would go leaving that excellent admonition hanging like an echo in the air.

Purifying is the work of the Holy Spirit, and the instrument he uses is the word of God. Didn't Jesus tell his disciples, *"Now ye are clean through the word which I have spoken unto you?"* [5]

When Jesus, nearing the end of his earthly ministry, prayed to the Father on the behalf of his disciples he said,

> *"I have given them thy word; and the world hath hated them, because they are not of the world, even as I am not of the world. I pray not that thou shouldest take them out of the world, but that thou shouldest keep them from the evil. They are not of the world, even as I am not of the world. Sanctify them through the truth: thy word is truth. As thou hast sent me into the world, even so have I also sent them into the world. And for their sakes I sanctify myself, that they also might be sanctified through the truth. Neither pray I for these alone, but for them also which shall believe on me through their word."* [6]

It is the truth of the word that sets the regenerated believer apart from the world, sanctifies him to the Lord, and purifies him, making him a vessel unto honor. The same word that purifies the saint has power to convict the sinner. The cry of David's heart was, *"Make me to understand the way of thy precepts: so shall I talk of thy wondrous works."* [7]

Surely Timothy would recognize the correlation between the

word that David loved and was directed by and the Living Word that is his Lord and the seed of David. It is through the knowledge of His word that we gain knowledge of the Lord himself; and it is through the right preaching of that word that others come to know him, too.

Timothy's instructions are clear, "*Study to show thyself approved unto God.*" Paul is not advising him to enroll in a seminary or take a course in theology. Of the three times the word "study" appears in our English Bible, only once does it refer to academics.[8] In both of the other incidents it simply means to give diligence to the matter at hand. In this case, "Give diligence to show yourself approved unto God, a workman that needs not to be ashamed, handling the word of God correctly."

Every potential servant of God has access to that which will make him mature, complete and thoroughly equipped for every good work. Later in this same letter Paul explains to Timothy that

> "*All scripture is given by inspiration of God, and is profitable for doctrine, for reproof, for correction, for instruction in righteousness: that the man of God may be perfect, throughly furnished unto all good works.*"[9]

What a treasure we have in our Bible! Every word is inspired by God. Obviously not everyone who professes to be a child of God is convinced of that or there would be no debate about the truth, accuracy or reliability of its content. But if one would be effective and minister with power, he must be persuaded that the scripture is the inspired word of God.

He must also be convinced that it is profitable enough for him to invest a part of every day reading it in order to absorb its content and be instructed by its wisdom. It is profitable for doctrine; that is, what God thinks and wants to teach us. It is profitable for reproof; that is, to reveal our errors and show us where we are wrong. It is profitable for correction; that is, to show us how to rectify our errors so that we are useable and effective. And it is profitable to instruct us in righteousness so that we can grow up day by day into the fullness of Christ. He has given us his word in order that we might be mature and complete and perfectly equipped for every good work. There is no other source from which we might obtain that benefit.

One way or another the servant of the Lord is a preacher of the word. To preach effectively he must be purified; but what purifying agent is present if he neglects the word of God? He needs to be empowered; but what good thing does the Spirit of God find to empower in him apart from the word of God?

Shun the Profane and the Vain

Unless one is involved as Paul was in the conflict between light and darkness, it is difficult to discern what damage Adam's fall wrought upon the world. It may seem to us that it is a place full of good things to be enjoyed, bad things to be avoided and loads of neutral things that matter little one way or the other. As time passes, that neutral category gradually expands to include more and more of the things that once were considered bad.

As the bar is lowered, what was once shocking is considered entertaining; what was once filthy becomes funny. And since fun and entertainment are now considered tax-deductible essentials to our modern lifestyle "it should be evident that they have no debilitating effect on the character of our society." Thus we sanitize our corruption and rationalize our behavior.

Language is the main device in making these adjustments in our collective value system. Words mean something. They vibrate upon our eardrums simply as sound waves; but beyond that point they translate into permanent contributors to thought patterns that affect judgments and decisions, which in turn govern our behavior. Their effect is either positive or negative.

Through Adam's fall corruption prevailed. As a farmer he waged a losing battle; the earth brought forth thorns and weeds to choke the good fruits of his labor. Noxious weeds abound in the earth and in a spiritual counterpart noxious words abound; corrupt communication prevails in this system called "the world." Lies contend with truth. The atmosphere is filled with words, and none are neutral in their effect. In varying degrees every one of them is either constructive or corrosive. As a servant of the Lord Timothy must understand this; and if you and I will be soldiers in God's service it is imperative that we understand the total effectiveness of what our words communicate to either substantiate or subvert.

Since we know that *God is able to do exceeding abundantly above all that we ask or think, according to the power that works in us,*[10] it seems apparent that there is more going on than we have consciously thought about, had anything to do with implementing or are able to observe. Therefore it is beyond our ability to govern the effect of our efforts, which are greater than we may imagine; but what we can control is the nature and quality of our contribution. Hymanæus and Philetus taught error and contributed what amounted to spiritual cancer, undermining and overthrowing the faith of those that heard them.

There is something Paul defines as profane and vain babblings. "Profane" is a word used to signify something secular, common, unsanctified or unholy. Ezekiel's temple in Jerusalem, for example, is considered holy, and into it will come only Jews because they are considered a holy people. On the outside is a courtyard where the Gentiles are allowed. This area is considered "profane." That doesn't mean it is a wicked place, but it is not a holy place. Profane, therefore, may refer to something considered innocuous in character, but that has no connection to anything holy.[11]

"Vain" describes anything vacuous, that is, without intellectual content, that serves no useful purpose, or is nonsensical. It is the form of communication that Paul had admonished the Ephesian believers against when he told them to put away foolish talking and inconvenient jesting.[12] This form of levity may seem harmless because although it adds nothing to our spiritual stature, as far as we can see, neither does it subtract.

"Not so," says Paul. "Shun profane and vain babblings: for they will increase unto *more* ungodliness." Obviously there can only be *more* of something that was there to begin with. In the smallest increments profane and vain babblings are ungodly and they will increase unto yet more ungodliness. Nothing is neutral. If the word of God builds faith, that which distracts from or opposes it destroys faith.

It has been suggested that these remarks imply that there is no place for humor in our communications. Nothing could be farther from the truth. I'm sure humor is God-given. Nonsense and jesting that is harmful is inappropriate—or as Paul said, inconvenient. This may include hurtful ridicule, snide remarks and joking that makes impurity something to be laughed at. As was earlier pointed out, however, a healthy sense of humor is an enormous asset, especially when circumstances are particularly trying. A keen wit is often the means of defusing a tense situation, or bringing some sunlight into a dark moment. The animal kingdom seems to reveal that even God has a sense of humor. When you watch the antics of a baby almost anything, it seems you can almost hear Him laughing.

We may learn good things from negative experiences. Sometimes our failings teach us more than our successes. We are walking in righteousness today because we have learned the folly of the unrighteousness in which we walked before, and from which we have now repented. We have no desire to return, but if we are inclined to lend our ears to that which does not edify, it becomes increasingly easy to be partakers in vain conversations, and more difficult to avoid them.

Criticism can become a bad habit; easy to acquire but hard to break. Like a narcotics addiction, it is subtle. One gains quickly the habit of evil speaking. It can blunt our testimony, devastate our prayer life, and diminish our zeal for proclaiming the truth. It is like a fountain sending forth sweet and bitter water from the same spring. Solomon said it this way:

> *"For a dream cometh through the multitude of business; and a fool's voice is known by multitude of words."* [13] *"In the multitude of words there wanteth not sin: but he that refraineth his lips is wise."*[14]

Criticism is the pronouncement of a judgment we have made about someone. It is quite possibly false; but even if true, it is outside our jurisdiction. When we have pronounced our judgment, it automatically and instantly colors, to some degree, the estimate of the hearer about the one being criticized. It militates against unity in the church and sows discord among the brethren. This, then, is a serious matter because listed among things God hates are *a false witness that speaketh lies, and he that soweth discord among brethren.* [15]

> **19 *Nevertheless the foundation of God standeth sure, having this seal, the Lord knoweth them that are his. And let everyone that nameth the name of Christ depart from iniquity 20 But in a great house there are not only vessels of gold and of silver, but also of wood and of earth; and some to honor, and some to dishonor. 21 If a man therefore purge himself from these, he shall be a vessel unto honor, sanctified and meet for the master's use, and prepared unto every good work.***

It's a good thing the Lord knows who his people are because we can't always tell. There are saints whose names are recorded in scripture that were not always saintly; men whom the Lord acknowledged as his own that sometimes brought reproach upon his name. David comes to mind who committed adultery with Bathsheba, and Solomon who instituted idolatry in Jerusalem; Peter, who denied the Lord, and even after the day of Pentecost played the hypocrite at Antioch and was rebuked by Paul.[16] Many are the incidents throughout history when otherwise godly men followed their flesh and acted no differently from their ungodly counterparts.

There are also ungodly people that have presented such a righteous appearance that they have been mistaken for saints. Man can only look on the outward appearance, but the Lord looks upon the heart. That verse in 1 Samuel 16:7 has often been quoted to prove that the outward appearance is insignificant because, although man looks there, the Lord doesn't. He sees what's in the heart and that's all that matters. That isn't true. Our outward appearance and our outward behavior should be an accurate representation of what God sees when he looks upon the heart. To see what God sees in the heart, men have no alternative but to look at the outward appearance. They should be the same.

When Paul wrote to the Romans he rebuked the religious Jews among them, saying,

> *"Thou that makest thy boast of the law, through breaking the law dishonorest thou God? For the name of God is blasphemed among the Gentiles through you, as it is written."* [17]

And now he is writing Timothy to impress upon him how extremely important it is that his words and his behavior verify his profession of faith. In matters small and great this must be a guiding principle. In our benign society, if you display a fish symbol or a Christian bumper sticker on your car, you need to drive well and obey the law. Your action should convey the same testimony that your insignia implies. In the hostile environment that much of the church around the world endures, if you profess to know the Lord, you need to stand courageously and steadfast in the face of opposition or even persecution. There is no alternative to this; the Gospel is either preached or profaned. Behavior, like words, is either positive or negative in its effect. Nothing is neutral. You either verify the Gospel or you vilify it.

The church is a great house filled with vessels of various fashion fitted for varying types of service. Some seem ornamental; gold and silver vessels with apparently opulent roles to fill. Others are utilitarian, fulfilling functional purposes without celebrity or, oftentimes, even recognition; simple wooden or earthen vessels indispensable to the function of the great house. Whether gold, silver, wood or earth they are either honorable or dishonorable depending on how they are employed. It is better to be an honorable earthen vessel than a golden vessel of dishonor. *"If a man therefore purge himself from 'these,' he shall be a vessel unto honor."*

"These" are what Paul has already condemned: words that subvert the hearer, profane and vain babblings that increase to more ungodliness, error that overthrows faith, and iniquity that belies the testimony of some who name the name of Christ. Purge yourself from that which makes you a vessel unto dishonor and you will be a vessel unto honor, "sanctified, and meet for the master's use, and prepared unto every good work." There is no way to be better equipped than that.

Earthen vessels are not admonished to become vessels of gold; or wooden vessels to become vessels of silver. One is not more useful to the master than the other. But a vessel of dishonor, whether golden or earthen, is of no advantage at all in the master's house.

Examples of such vessels abound in scripture. Perhaps the kings of Israel would be considered vessels of gold. Among them were vessels to honor such as David, Hezekiah and Josiah; and others to dishonor such as Saul, Ahab and Joash. The earthen vessels may represent lesser lights of lower station some of whom we may have never heard. But among them were those to honor and those to dishonor. It may well be that God's estimate of whom gold and silver represent, and who are those of wood and earth, is quite different from ours. The point is, However, that we must not strive to change our station, envy or try to imitate someone that we think has a greater role: Our responsibility is to be, through purity, humility and submission to our Lord, vessels of honor.

> **22 Flee also youthful lusts; but follow righteousness, faith, charity, peace, with them that call on the Lord out of a pure heart.**

There is such a thing as courage, and there is such a thing as wisdom. Sometimes retreat is a better strategy than fighting. A navy destroyer man once told me, "He who strikes and runs away, will live to strike another day." There are times when avoiding the struggle is a much wiser course than trying to fight it. Dealing with youthful lusts is one of those times.

Within every normal youth are desires that urge them to pursue adulthood. Dreams of independence, of being married and having a family, the desire to pursue a career and achieve success. Included in the mix are sexual desires and thoughts of material possessions; all of which are normal and healthy if guided aright and under control of the Spirit. If unfettered or misguided, these same desires have a dark potential. The world is continually appealing to these desires and offering shortcuts to gratify them by following the course of this world, at which time those healthy desires become fleshly lusts. Healthy sexual desires out of control and without restraint can turn to fornication. Healthy desires for financial or business success if misguided can turn into serving mammon.

Sometimes young people display indignation when an elder restrains them from situations that would put them at risk for temptations or moral challenges that may prove overwhelming.

Their reaction may be, "You don't trust me," or something equivalent.

If you are that elder your response should be, "You're right; I don't. I understand human nature and I know what the scriptures say about the matter. Neither should you trust yourself." There are reasons for applying propriety to our actions in situations that could present temptations to our flesh.

In our youth, necessary parameters, for which there should be no apology, are established by godly parents. They are meant to establish values and knowledge of what is right. As the youth enters adulthood, it is up to him to maintain godly values and recognize the parameters that God has set for him. Our flesh may kick against the Spirit's restraint, but if we walk in the Spirit, we will not fulfill the lusts of the flesh.[18]

Youthful lusts come in different packages. Some, as we have discussed are packaged as sin, i.e. fornication, love of money, etc. Others come in more cheerful, harmless-looking wrappers, like "fun," laziness, irresponsibility and such things as seem to be excusable in youth. It seems in each successive generation these things are excused for a longer time; maturity seems to be coming later these days.

There were, at one time, children and adults. The transition was made relatively quickly. Timothy, for example, was probably a youth of about seventeen years when he was enjoying a reputation "of good report," and Paul chose him to be a team member. But at some time in the recent past someone invented the "teen-ager," who, in the mind of many was expected to be irresponsible, independent and unreliable. Not all young people in their teen years are willing to fit that description, and among them are some remarkably mature and successful individuals. But among that class of "teen-agers" that have been allowed to meet the aforementioned low expectations, there is an increasing inclination to remain irresponsible on into the twenties and, in some cases even into the thirties. This is a serious problem stemming from a lack of discipline.

The world beckons constantly to those who are willing to entertain the thought, "Come and play; neglect responsibility, relax, don't take life seriously. Come do what everyone else is doing. The warfare is not that serious, nor the commission that urgent. Come enjoy your youth." God's word still urges us to flee youthful lusts.

To those who would serve the Lord the command is clear, "*Flee youthful lusts.*" That's not all; the escape route is specific, "*Follow righteousness, faith, charity, peace, with them that call on the Lord out of a pure heart.*" We cannot simply run away from temptation, we must pursue righteousness, and we must do it with likeminded saints. There are no supermen among us who, by the heroics of their flesh can be victorious over their flesh. God has told us that the flesh and the spirit are contrary to one another. It is when we walk in the Spirit that we do not fulfill the lusts of the flesh.[19] And that is not meant to be a lonesome and isolated path unless by the Lord's design for a while he has made it so. We are to assemble with other believers in order that we can admonish and encourage one another, and the more often and the more diligently as we see the darkening days of the end time approaching.

> **23** *But foolish and unlearned questions avoid, knowing that they do gender strifes.* **24** *And the servant of the Lord must not strive; but be gentle unto all men, apt to teach, patient,* **25** *In meekness instructing those that oppose themselves; if God peradventure will give them repentance to the acknowledging of the truth;* **26** *And that they may recover themselves out of the snare of the devil, who are taken captive by him at his will.*

There is no record in the New Testament of the Lord Jesus arguing with his opponents. He reproved them, rebuked them and enlightened them, but he never strove with them. Paul likewise was often opposed by his many detractors resulting in his defense of his ministry, but he did not involve himself in contentious wrangling or fruitless debate. This is an important fact for one who is entrusted to take a message as important as the Gospel to a world that by its nature is opposed to truth. What better way is there to detract from the dignity and power of the Gospel than to entangle the messenger in discussing meaningless trivia? How many times have weighty discourses been aborted by the injection of some unrelated nonsense?

A typical incident of this occurred one day as we preached the Gospel on a college campus. One of our team had engaged a young man in a meaningful dialogue and had managed to keep the conversation centered on the Gospel despite several questions that could have sidetracked it. Soon, another member of our party sat down with the two to listen. Once more the University student brought up an unrelated question to which the newcomer felt compelled to respond. Soon the foolish and unlearned question became the center of an unfruitful discussion that displaced any further witness of the Gospel and an opportunity was lost.

This does not mean that simple but sincere questions should not be answered. On the contrary, many obstacles to believing have been removed by a judicious answer to a simple question. If we would be apt to teach, we must be ready to listen. If we would pave the way to faith, we must be ready and willing to address those things that lie as hindrances in the way. Some of the simplest things are the most efficient barriers to repentance and faith. The sincerity of the questioner is frequently what determines whether a question is simple or foolish.

It is frequently from intellectuals that foolish and unlearned questions emanate. Their questions are not for information, but for contention. Peter made mention in his second epistle of those who are willingly ignorant,[20] which means that though they know better, they deliberately adopt a position contrary to the truth. Peter illustrates who these people are by using as an example those that oppose the doctrine of creation.

Even though they are fools who present themselves as learned and are contentious, they are not beyond redemption. It is not they that must be avoided, but their foolish and unlearned questions, because they gender arguments. Paul did not tell Timothy that the servant of the Lord *should* not strive; he was more emphatic than that. This is an imperative; he *must* not strive. Contrariwise he must be gentle unto all men. Such a reaction does not always come naturally, and it is not always easy to respond gently to a contentious opponent, but it is what is prescribed for God's servants. We have as evidence the Lord himself,

> *"Who when he was reviled, reviled not again; when he suffered, he threatened not; but committed himself to him that judgeth righteously."* [21]

The servant of the Lord must be apt to teach and patient. Both "teach" and "patient" imply a time factor. Teaching is a process, normally not instantaneous; it means applying line upon line, precept upon precept until there is a foundation upon which faith can rest. Patience implies the endurance of frustrations that arise, perhaps, through the need to repeat things that should be readily grasped and easily retained.

Solomon taught us that "*A soft answer turneth away wrath: but grievous words stir up anger.*" [22] He said also, "*Only by pride cometh contention: but with the well advised is wisdom.*" [23] So when Paul instructed Timothy to demonstrate meekness when he instructs those that set themselves in opposition, he was echoing Solomon's counsel. Contention begets contention, anger stirs up anger, and meekness produces a reaction conducive to receiving instruction. Those who reject the truth are taken captive by Satan at his will, but when God moves upon them to change their mind they are able to recover themselves out of the snare of the devil.

(Endnotes)

[1] Psalm 119:111
[2] Psalm 119:4,5
[3] Psalm 119:103
[4] Psalm 119:9-11
[5] John 15:3
[6] John 17:14-20
[7] Psalm 119:27
[8] Ecclesiastes 12:12
[9] 2 Timothy 3:16,17
[10] Ephesians 3:20
[11] Ezekiel 42:20; 48:15
[12] Ephesians 5:3,4
[13] Ecclesiastes 5:3
[14] Proverbs 10:19
[15] Proverbs 6:19
[16] Galatians 2:11-14
[17] Romans 2:23,24
[18] Galatians 5:16
[19] ibid.
[20] 2 Peter 3:5
[21] 1 Peter 2:23
[22] Proverbs 15:1
[23] Proverbs 13:10

Chapter 6

Perilous Times

3:1 *This know also, that in the last days perilous times shall come. 2 For men shall be lovers of their own selves, covetous, boasters, proud, blasphemers, disobedient to parents, unthankful, unholy, 3 Without natural affection, trucebreakers, false accusers, incontinent, fierce, despisers of those that are good, 4 Traitors, heady, highminded, lovers of pleasures more than lovers of God; 5 Having a form of godliness, but denying the power thereof: from such turn away. 6 For of this sort are they that creep into houses, and lead captive silly women laden with sins, led away with divers lusts, 7 Ever learning, and never able to come to the knowledge of the truth.*

The day in which Paul wrote this letter to Timothy was historically a perilous time. Men perished or were preserved at the whim of a totalitarian ruler. Paul himself was condemned for no just reason, and even as he wrote this epistle his life hung in the balance. There have always been corrupt rulers, and there will always be men unjustly condemned. Paul, in his reference to perilous times to come

93

was speaking of a time of phenomenal and universal immorality that would transcend previous levels. Mankind, since the fall of Adam, has always been corrupt; but Paul contended that evil men would wax worse and worse. [1]

It cannot be said that Paul was a pessimist. How could he have been and still kept a joyful perspective with execution staring him in the face? Paul was an eternal optimist looking at everything in the light of the hope that was laid up for him in heaven. However, concerning this world and its future, he was a realist. In preparing Timothy for what lay before him he had to tell it like it is. Time has proved him right. It has all come upon us so incrementally, though, that we have hardly noticed that right has become wrong and that darkness has become light.[2]

Gradually, things have changed. Values have been reversed so that what was once considered "bedrock" to a sound society has become unusual or exceptional. Men have become lovers of their own selves, covetous, boasters, proud. How could it not be so? Where once we were taught to "*do unto others as you would have them do unto you,*" [3] now we are taught to "look out for number one." When Paul said men would be lovers of themselves, he was warning of a bad thing. Now, even in the church, we are taught that to love self is a good thing, an absolute necessity if we are to be psychologically healthy. "If you don't love yourself first," we are told, "you can't love anyone else."

Jesus said, "*He that loveth his life shall lose it.*" [4] Paul concurred when he taught,

> "*We are the circumcision, which worship God in the Spirit, rejoice in Christ Jesus, and have no confidence in the flesh...what things were gain for me, those I counted loss for Christ.*" [5]

Those principles, even when applied to business and commerce assure success. Paul taught servants, even slaves, to look out for their masters' interests;[6] and he taught masters to look out for the interests of their servants.[7] When applied, that concept has built strong economies and prosperous businesses. But greed and self-serving bring those successes to an end. When the labor force begins to exploit capital, as is so common in a socially minded society, they "kill the goose that lays the golden egg." Or when capital begins to exploit labor, which is what can happen when human nature begins to corrupt a capitalistic system, a "cancer" develops that destroys the harmony of mutual cooperation. Labor without capital is frustrated, and capital without labor is immobilized. Greed, pride and self-love will ultimately bring destruction to any system and render it subject to the control of the basest of men. The last days will be epitomized by just such a condition, which we are witnessing in this new century. This is the fruit of the doctrine of self-love.

This elevation of the flesh has even more dire consequences. Ultimately, in the end of this progression, a man of sin will

> *"oppose and exalt himself above all that is called God, or that is worshipped; so that he as God [will sit] in the temple of God, showing himself that he is God."* [8]

That will not happen in a vacuum: it is the epitome of what is happening already. As man is taught to elevate himself, he sees less need for God. Already we have arrived at this age of blasphemy.

"God did not create the heaven and the earth," say the grade school teachers to our little ones, and the high school teachers to our adolescents, and the college professors to our young adults. "It all came about by itself."

"A higher power, perhaps; but must we call him God?" say the psychologists. "Religion is superstition, the higher power is within you, and it is your self esteem."

Atheist societies have formed to evangelize the nation and "deliver" the next generation from the bondage of religion, setting them free from the superstitions of their parents. These are blasphemers fostering a society that is unthankful, unholy, disobedient to parental authority and other established authority as well.

Is there any doubt about the accuracy of Paul's prediction that the last days would see men and women without natural affection?

Television stations blatantly air pornographic programs during prime time; messages that would convince any viewer that virginity at almost any age is an idea from the dark ages. Recreational sex is for everyone: single, married, young or old. To think otherwise is, at the very least, naïve. As a consequence marriages are consummated without commitment, infidelity and divorce soon follow, families are decimated, bonds are broken and trusts violated.

Since marriage vows are no longer inviolable, marriage is denigrated and the term is applied even to homosexual relationships. Whatever satiates the lust of the flesh is acceptable, and to stand in opposition to this unnatural behavior is to be branded a bigot.

Children, which were at one time the expected and desired fruit of a marriage relationship are today, to a large segment of the population—including many in the church—an unplanned and unwanted by-product of a self-indulgent act; an inconvenience that will be disposed of with the trash. In the thirty-four years from 1973 to 2007 about fifty million of them were aborted. About 1.5 million a year, for the convenience, in most cases, of some parent without natural affection, were flushed down toilets or disposed of with the garbage.

Can there be any doubt that "lovers of pleasure more than lovers of God" applies to our present time? And yet, with all of this, church buildings are full. Mega churches continue to spring up with entertaining programs that draw thousands of people to buildings that cost millions of dollars. And while congregations grow, so does the sin tide rise in the nation both without and within those great assemblies. It seems that the more the religions flourish, the less influence they have upon the nation. As it was in the days of Noah, God's judgment waits for the final day.

Paul apparently expected Timothy to experience the days of which he wrote, and perhaps Timothy did see then what we are seeing now, but we can be sure that the longer it has gone on, the worse it has become. Paul advised his young coworker to turn away from religious practice that is characterized as form without power. Timothy is gone now, but the word that was written to him is still here, preserved for all of time in the canon of scripture. And we are here to read it as though it were written to us. It is as imperative for us to pay earnest attention to it as it was for Timothy. This is now our day and our battle; and if we are faithful as Paul was, it will be our crown.

> **6 *For of this sort are they which creep into houses, and lead captive silly women laden with sins, led away with divers lusts 7 Ever learning and never able to come to the knowledge of the truth. 8 Now as Jannes and Jambres withstood Moses, so do these also resist the truth: men of corrupt minds, reprobate concerning the faith. 9 But they shall proceed no further: for their folly shall be manifest to all men, as theirs also was.***

"This sort" is a reference to those who have a form of godliness but deny the power thereof. They are persons that value psychology and human reasoning above the pure word of God; that teach self-love rather than self-denial and the bearing of the cross. They are those who produce or promote movies and television programs that exalt promiscuity in sex, infidelity in marriage, and treat homosexuality as a benign alternative. They creep into homes by way of radio, television, magazines and all sorts of advertising, bringing the message of feminism, independence, self-indulgence, disobedience to parents and rebellion against the creator.

Much of this malignancy is disguised as education. "Science" programs make casual mention of happenings of billions of years ago. Such respected publications as National Geographic verify those dates as though they are established facts. As was already stated, this imaginative information is passed on to public schoolchildren from the very earliest grades and published in preschool children's books until it sounds so normal that talk of creation seems to be the aberrant text.

All of this was foreknown by the apostle Paul either by faith or by revelation from God or perhaps by what had already begun in his time. He had written in his first letter to Timothy,

> *"O Timothy, keep that which is committed to thy trust, avoiding profane and vain babblings, and oppositions of science falsely so called; which some professing have erred from the faith."* [9]

This corruption is embraced not only by ignorant and untutored souls and the silly women who are led easily astray, but by men of letters who are ever learning and ever teaching but never able to come to the knowledge of the truth. Much of what they learn is fallacious and what they teach is falsely described as science. And not all of these teachers are secular. Many religious teachers are among their number. These are often men regarded as wise and spiritually powerful men of faith who have large followings and are relied upon to uphold truth.

Such men were Jannes and Jambres who withstood Moses. It is commonly understood that these two were among the wise men and magicians that Pharaoh called upon when Moses and Aaron came to him to demand the release of the children of Israel from their bondage.[10] Their effect was to negate the work of the Holy Spirit that was demonstrated through Moses and Aaron. Aaron cast the rod of Moses on the ground before Pharaoh and it miraculously became a serpent. Then the magicians cast their rods upon the ground in the same place before the same audience, and in a miraculous display apparently no different from that of God's prophets, their rods became serpents. Those were swallowed up by Moses' rod, but beyond that, in Pharaoh's estimation the power of Jehovah did not exceed the power of his Egyptian gods.

So it is today, religious practice or secular knowledge seems to compete favorably with the truth of God's word; to many it seems even greater and more impressive. Therefore those who rely on sight, feeling or mere intellectual stimulation will not embrace the truth. Ultimately, however, their folly will be made known to all men.

> **10** *But thou hast fully known my doctrine, manner of life, purpose, faith, longsuffering, charity, patience,* **11** *Persecutions, afflictions, which came unto me at Antioch, at Iconium, at Lystra; what persecutions I endured: but out of them all the Lord delivered me.* **12** *Yea, and all that will live godly in Christ Jesus shall suffer persecution.* **13** *But evil men and seducers shall wax worse and worse, deceiving and being deceived.*

Paul's example is in total contrast to those men that he previously described and to the evil men and seducers waxing ever worse. What makes the difference? The first were men of corrupt minds, driven by lust and seeking carnal companionship with those who were likewise driven. It is the difference between the reprobate mind of reprobate men, and the mind of Christ that ruled the conduct of this godly apostle. This also defines the difference between the sons of Adam, citizens of this world system and those who are sons of God by virtue of the rebirth that has made us citizens of heaven.

What a privileged life Timothy had endured and enjoyed for the past decade and a half. Even though Paul claimed to be rude in speech [11] and there were others who thought his speech contemptible,[12] it was an education like no other for Timothy to hear from this apostle's mouth "all the counsel of God" [13] as he preached the Gospel and instructed the saints in every place.

We also have access to that counsel, because the doctrine that Timothy heard has been preserved for us to read in the epistles of Paul that comprise much of our New Testament. We are ill served if we fail to take advantage of the divinely inspired information that has been recorded there. Each of Paul's fourteen epistles was written to address a specific need and with the letters of the other apostles and the Gospels, the saints are fully informed.

For over fifteen years Timothy has been immersed in Paul's doctrine and shared his life. He knows the purpose that has driven Paul and the faith that has sustained him; he has experienced his love and marveled at his patience in unbelievably difficult situations and unbearable contradictions. Paul has been a model of godly consistency and fortitude. He has not changed directions even in the most discouraging circumstances. That's his point: such trials are not unexpected for a soldier; such challenges must not make us flee or turn aside. You saw it, Timothy. Now you are called upon to follow. It's part of the course. Yea, all that will live godly in Christ Jesus shall suffer persecution.

Now he talks about all that will live godly in Christ Jesus. Surely that includes you and me. It must if it is our purpose to serve God. We don't want to miss Paul's meaning here. "All" means everyone, none excluded. "Will" means "fully intends to." If it is our purpose to live godly in Christ Jesus, for that determination there is a promised consequence. We shall—that is an inescapable certainty—suffer persecution. And it does not appear that this prospect will become less of a probability as time goes by. The statement that evil men and seducers will grow worse is prophetic and with time the deceived and the deceivers will increase.

What can we possibly make of this? Does it seem to you that the battle we are enduring is worse than the one Paul was embroiled in? On the contrary, it seems our lives today are relatively peaceful; persecution is a word we seldom hear and barely understand. Our churches are full and function freely, our speech is not censored. Everything seems fine from here. God bless America! Besides, it's ski season, or hunting season, or fishing season, and I'm a little too busy to think about all this stuff right now.

Actually, though, there are some things that are a little disturbing and may distract a little from the fun stuff. The economy is down and the stock market is unstable, even falling. My bottom line was a little weak this month compared to last, and the price of gas is killing me. I really do have important things to think about; so don't bother me with this "persecution" stuff and deceivers, etc. As soon as we get through this downturn, everything will be as it has always been.

100

The deception is strong; and the prevailing complacency is the evidence that it is strong. It is obvious to those who are in the word and comparing the present world scene to what they are reading there, that everything is not all right. Many saints around the world are suffering at the hands of persecutors for the very reasons that Paul has described. Perhaps the reason we are experiencing little persecution is because there is little will to live godly in Christ Jesus. The world does not perceive the traditional church to be its opponent. There is little discernment among many saints of how deeply the philosophies and the values of this world have dominated the minds of professing Christians and even the message of their churches.

That, of course, is not true of all. There are those—and it is not a few—that, burdened for the church and for the nation, intercede continually for revival among God's people and for conviction of sin for those who are not His people. They pray that God's judgments, which surely must come, will be withheld for a while longer. But still, for those who will live godly, there shall be persecution. Let us not avoid it by relinquishing our will. As it increases, may our will to live godly in Christ Jesus be increasingly firm.

> **14 But continue thou in the things which thou hast learned and hast been assured of, knowing of whom thou has learned them; 15 And that from a child thou hast known the holy scriptures, which are able to make thee wise unto salvation through faith which is in Christ Jesus. 16 All scripture is given by inspiration of God, and is profitable for doctrine, for reproof, for correction, for instruction in righteousness: 17 That the man of God may be perfect, throughly furnished unto all good works.**

The course of those who will live godly is fixed. Those who hear the Gospel preached fully and truthfully, being convicted by the Holy Spirit of sin, righteousness and judgment, repent toward God and place their faith in the Lord Jesus Christ. They are made the righteousness of God in Christ and become new creatures. It is not as though they merely make an intellectual decision to turn over a new leaf and adopt a different philosophical idea and from that point on try to live on a higher plane. There is nothing in that to generate power to swim upstream, or even to make one know which direction is upstream.

Jesus, praying to the Father said,

"Sanctify them through thy word; thy word is truth."

The Holy Scriptures that Timothy had known from his childhood gave him wisdom to put his faith in Christ for salvation. But there is something more about those scriptures of which Paul wanted to remind Timothy, although undoubtedly he was already fully aware. This letter, Paul knew, was destined to find its way to the eyes of many generations beyond this young man. Your eyes and mine and those of all the saints inhabiting these last days are the target of these words.

Over fifty-seven years ago, as a twenty-three-year-old young man I was convinced of the Gospel. The moment I confessed that I had received the new birth, the young man who was with me and witnessed my salvation asked me, "Would you like to be perfect?"

I emphatically replied, "Yes I would."

"Would you like to be equipped for every good work?" He asked.

Again my response was a definite, "Yes."

"Then read this," he said, holding before me his Bible opened to this very scripture, 2 Timothy 3:16,17. "All scripture," he pointed out, "means the whole Bible. The Old Testament and the New; the exciting parts and the parts that seem dry and hard to understand. All of them are good for these four things: doctrine, which means the teaching God wants you to learn; reproof, which means telling you when you're wrong; correction, which means telling you how to make it right; and then instruction in righteousness so that you will know how to live every day."

He held it there while I read it aloud.

Then he said, "Read it every day all your life. It will equip you for every good work into which God might lead you. It will make you mature and complete. It's all the equipment you will ever need."

I am so thankful for that counsel. Even after many years I find it is true. I in turn have passed it on to many others.

(Endnotes)

[1] 2 Timothy 3:13
[2] Isaiah 5:20-23
[3] Matthew 7:12; Luke 6:31
[4] Luke 9:24
[5] Philippians 3:3
[6] Ephesians 6:5-8
[7] Ephesians 6:9
[8] 2 Thessalonians 2:4
[9] 1 Timothy 6:20,21
[10] Exodus 7:8-13
[11] 2 Corinthians 11:6
[12] 2 Corinthians 10:10
[13] Acts 20:27

Chapter 7

Preach The Word

4:1 I *charge thee therefore before God, and the Lord Jesus Christ, who shall judge the quick and the dead at his appearing and his kingdom; 2 Preach the word; be instant in season, out of season; reprove, rebuke, exhort with all longsuffering and doctrine.*

In the entire universe there is no power equal to that of the word. In the beginning the worlds were framed by the word of God.[1] All things are held together by that same word.[2] And it was that word that was made flesh and dwelt among us in the person of the Lord Jesus Christ.[3] He who is God

> *"made himself of no reputation, and took upon him the form of a servant, and was made in the likeness of men: and being found in fashion as a man, he humbled himself, and became obedient unto death, even the death of the cross."* [4]

The death that he experienced was ours, precipitated by the sin that passed upon all men because all have sinned.[5] Because God was not willing that any should perish, He judged our sin in the person of His Son,

> *"Who himself bare our sins in his own body on the tree,*
> *that we, being dead to sins should live unto righteousness."* [6]

This is where the rubber meets the road. This is why Timothy must preach the word when it is convenient, when it is not convenient; when people are amenable to listen and when they are not so inclined. Christ took us to the cross. He executed the old man in you and me so that we, being dead to sins, should live unto righteousness. Dead men are finished with their sin: they are finished with the allurements of this world. Raised with Christ they are free and responsible to live unto righteousness; they do not have a free pass to live according to their flesh. *And every one of us shall give account of himself to God.* [7]

Most of the world is ignorant of a coming judgment and many who are not, treat the subject with scorn. Among believers there is little discussion of the matter because we understand, and rightly so, that God placed upon Jesus the judgment that would have meant for us eternal damnation, making us instead his sons and daughters. Perhaps we are inclined to forget that even God's children are accountable. Did not Peter say that *judgment begins at the house of God*? [8]

Jesus spoke of judgment as well as blessing. But it seems there is a tendency to major on the positive promises and fail to see that the warnings are promises as well. The judgment of which Paul spoke to Timothy included the quick—that is the living—as well as the dead. The Word clothed Himself with humanity in order that he might be tempted in every way that we are, and that he could die as a mortal man—something that immortal Deity could not do—and that he could judge us from the perspective of perfect humanity.

> *Jesus said, "For the Father judgeth no man, but hath committed all judgment unto the Son:...For as the Father hath life in himself; so hath he given unto the Son to have life in himself; and he hath given him authority to execute judgment also, because he is the Son of Man."* [9]

Jesus during his earthly ministry was man as God meant man to be. He lived the life God meant man to live, and it is by that standard that man will be judged. God's word speaks of two judgments: one of the quick, or living; and one of the dead.

The delineation between these two is defined very concisely by the apostle John:

> *"And this is the record, that God hath given to us eternal life, and this life is in his Son. He that hath the Son hath life; and he that hath not the Son of God hath not life."* [10]

The judgments that these will experience are significantly different, but no less serious. Jesus taught his disciples about them even while he was making his way to the cross:

> *"He added and spake a parable, because he was nigh to Jerusalem, and because they thought that the kingdom of God should immediately appear."* [11]

They thought, as many do today, that following Jesus would lead them directly and painlessly to the kingdom of God. They were Jews and they knew what the scriptures say. The Messiah would come and establish his throne in Jerusalem from where he would rule over his kingdom. Obviously the time had come: Jesus the messiah was approaching Jerusalem and when he arrived there, the kingdom would immediately appear and they would rule and reign with him. But they were missing a major ingredient of the message—the cross, the resurrection and the suffering they must endure. Thus the parable.

He said therefore,

> *"A certain nobleman went into a far country to receive for himself a kingdom, and to return. And he called his ten servants, and delivered them ten pounds, and said unto them, 'Occupy till I come.'*
>
> *"But his citizens hated him, and sent a message after him, saying, 'We will not have this man to reign over us.'*
>
> *"And it came to pass, that when he was returned, having received the kingdom, then he commanded these servants to be called unto him, to whom he had given the money, that he might know how much every man had gained by*

trading.

"Then came the first saying, 'Lord, thy pound hath gained ten pounds.'

"And he said unto him, 'Well thou good servant: because thou hast been faithful in a very little, have thou authority over ten cities.'

"And the second came saying, 'Lord, thy pound hath gained five pounds.'

"And he said likewise to him, 'Be thou also over five cities.'

"And another came saying, 'Lord, behold, here is thy pound, which I have kept laid up in a napkin: for I feared thee, because thou art an austere man; thou takest up what thou layest not down, and reapest that thou didst not sow.'

"And he said unto him, 'Out of thine own mouth will I judge thee, thou wicked servant. Thou knewest that I was an austere man, taking up that I laid not down, and reaping that I did not sow; wherefore then gavest not thou my money into the bank, that at my coming I might have required mine own with usury?'

"And he said unto them that stood by, 'Take from him the pound, and give it to him that hath ten pounds.'

"And they said, 'Lord, he hath ten pounds.'

"For I say unto you, 'That unto every one which hath shall be given; and from him that hath not, even that he hath shall be taken away from him. But those mine enemies, which would not that I should reign over them, bring hither, and slay them before me.'

The nobleman is the Lord Jesus. The far country is the place to which the Lord Jesus ascended after His resurrection and after having given the commission to His disciples. The silver pounds are the word which he has given to His disciples in order to "occupy" or do His business until he returns. Those who hated Him constitute unbelieving Israel and all others who reject His authority.

He will return to establish his kingdom. When he comes, judgment will begin at the house of God. Every man will give account of himself to God. In the accounting, three things are in view: every man; how much each one gained; by trading. In the three examples he used, the two that pleased him and were rewarded made no reference to their own talent or ability; their claim was that his pound had produced the gain. They were judged and rewarded accordingly.

The third man expressed what he must have thought was a flattering opinion about his Lord's overbearing power, and boasted about what he had done to preserve the Lord's treasure. He had gained nothing and was judged and rewarded accordingly.

The kingdom is a thousand years during which time the saints will live with their rewards. Jesus impressed upon his disciples that the kingdom age will be, for those who have been faithful and fruitful, a marvelous time of ruling and reigning with him. But for those who have been unfaithful and unfruitful—as many even of those who boast of being the Lord's servants have been—it will be a millennium of regret and poverty.

We are not all apostles. We are not all Timothy; but the instruction given to Timothy applies also to us. Are we soldiers, as Paul instructed Timothy to be, unentangled with the affairs of this life? Are we athletes striving for the gold according to the rules? Are we farmers planting and sowing and partaking of the fruits?

We are vessels of gold, silver, wood or earth; but are we vessels unto honor? Are we meekly instructing those that set themselves in opposition to the truth so that God will perhaps give them repentance to the acknowledging of the truth in order that they that are taken captive by the devil may recover themselves out of his snare? That's our work. That's what "trading" represents.

> **3 *For the time will come when they will not endure sound doctrine; but after their own lusts shall they heap to themselves teachers, having itching ears; 4 And they shall turn away their ears from the truth, and shall be turned unto fables.***

You are reading Paul's letter to Timothy from the perspective of the twenty-first century. Perhaps that's an advantage; perhaps not. That would largely depend on the doctrine to which you have been exposed. Those who espouse the word that Timothy was charged with will have a different view of things than those whose ears have been filled with fables.

It is not those who consider themselves to be atheists, agnostics or simply infidels to whom Paul is referring, it is people that want their "truth" to be what they want to hear. They seek out teachers because, obviously, they want teaching. The teachers they want, however, are those that will tickle their ears and entertain them with pleasantries and promises of good things. Sound doctrine will repulse them. Perhaps it will sound too judgmental, or too rigid, or too scary, or too legalistic or not legalistic enough. Whatever it is, to them it will be objectionable; so they will turn away their ears from the truth and be turned unto fables. But all the while they may be under the illusion that they are counted among the "Christians." These are those days, and this is that generation.

We have moved a long way from what the early church was recognized to be. At that time it comprised born again believers, and therefore the church recognized its distinction from the world, which despised it. The church met for the purpose of encouraging the saints in their constant conflict with the world. The meeting was a means of edifying, not entertaining, one another. This edification was accomplished by every member of the assembly exercising his or her gift as the Holy Spirit directed. When the saints were inclined to be man-followers, the apostles rebuked them, pointing out that Jesus alone is the head of the body. The believers assembled with those in their locale. They did not have the "luxury" to pick and choose where they would "go to church" based on where the music was best, or the preacher most entertaining. Churches did not advertise their programs in order to trump that of the competitor down the street. It seems clear that our times are the days about which Paul was writing.

> **5** *But watch thou in all things, endure afflictions, do the work of an evangelist, make full proof of thy ministry,* **6** *For I am now ready to be offered, and the time of my departure is at hand.* **7** *I have fought a good fight, I have finished my course, I have kept the faith:* **8** *Henceforth there is laid up for me a crown of righteousness, which the Lord, the righteous judge, shall give me at that day: and not to me only, but unto all them also that love his appearing.*

There are many subtle snares designed to turn faithful men back. It has ever been so. Eve was tempted when, by the enchanting voice of the serpent, her attention was directed to the beautiful tree with its delightful fruit that was reputed to make one wise. All the ingredients for sin were in that attractive tree—It was good for food (the lust of the flesh), beautiful to look upon (lust of the eye), and desired to make one wise (the pride of life).[12] She ate and gave to her husband and he disobeyed the Lord, with a devastating result. King David was distracted by the lust of his eyes when he should have been on the battlefield, and he disobeyed the Lord. The young prophet from Judah that came to Israel to prophesy against Jeroboam's altar was distracted by an old prophet whose lie he listened to; he disobeyed the Lord and died for it.[13] Now Paul has been disappointed by the defection of many stalwart men who have listened to the distracting voice of the adversary causing them to flee in the face of persecution.

"Therefore Timothy," Paul writes, "Watch thou in all things. Be careful, keep your wits about you; recognize the subtleties of the enemy and his empty threats; steel yourself against the afflictions that may come, and be prepared to endure them. Keep on proclaiming the gospel, which is the power of God unto salvation unto everyone that will believe. This is our answer in perilous times to evil men and seducers as they wax worse and worse."

And it is ours, too, in this generation that we have inherited.

111

There is no other recourse for the servants of the Lord. To "make full proof of your ministry" means to do it with all your might, and to continue to the end. Don't be turned back.

Paul's voice was strong to the end. He is not expiring with a whimper, but with a shout of triumph. He is speaking as an Olympian that has won the gold. He strove for masteries; he did it lawfully, and now he sees himself leaving the stadium and mounting the podium to be crowned with a crown of righteousness at the hand of the Lord, the righteous judge. For Paul this is not the end, but the beginning of the eternal stage of his life. And he is beginning with a burst of victory.

This is not just for Paul; it is for Timothy too, and for you and me as well. It is for all those who love his appearing.

(Endnotes)
[1] Psalm 33:6,9; Genesis 1:1; John 1:1-3
[2] Hebrews 1:2,3
[3] John 1:14
[4] Philippians 2:7,8
[5] Romans 5:12
[6] 1 Peter 2:24
[7] Romans 14:12
[8] 1 Peter 4:17
[9] John 5:22-27
[10] 1 John 5:11,12
[11] Luke 19:11
[12] 1 John 2:15,16
[13] 1 Kings 13:11-26

Chapter 8

Defection and Discipleship

9 Do thy diligence to come shortly unto me: 10 For Demas hath forsaken me, having loved this present world, and is departed unto Thessalonica; Crescens to Galatia, Titus unto Dalmatia. 11 Only Luke is with me. Take Mark, and bring him with thee: for he is profitable to me for the ministry. 12 And Tychicus have I sent to Ephesus. 13 The cloak that I left at Troas with Carpus, when thou comest, bring with thee, and the books, but especially the parchments. 14 Alexander the coppersmith did me much evil: the Lord reward him according to his works: 15 Of whom be thou ware also; for he hath greatly withstood our words.

No doubt there are safer places for Timothy to be than visiting Paul in his prison, but safety is not the issue here. There is a need, and Timothy is in a position to meet it. There are books and parchments that Paul has left in various places that would be helpful in whatever he is doing now. It is probable that these things have contributed to the New Testament which we now read. Continuing to minister must have been difficult—perhaps nearly impossible. Others had quit but that was not an option for Paul.

Demas, who with Luke had accompanied Paul as a faithful fellow-laborer, had continued with him during his first imprisonment. This time, however, the situation appeared more serious, even life threatening. Perhaps when he realized that to continue could cost his life, he was not ready for that so he departed having loved this present world. Crescens and Titus also left, one to Galatia, the other to Dalmatia. It is not clear whether they defected, as Demas obviously had, or if Paul dispatched them to minister in those places as he had apparently sent Tychicus to Ephesus. We would hope it was the latter case, but there are some details we don't know for sure.

Luke, the beloved physician as Paul had described him in his letter to the Colossians,[1] remained faithful to the end and gave us the Gospel according to Luke and the Acts of the Apostles, both of which are indispensable parts of our New Testament giving us rich insight into the life and ministry of the Lord Jesus and the beginnings of the early church age.

The name of the apostle Barnabas is not mentioned in this letter, but Paul's request that Mark be brought to Rome is a remarkable tribute to him and his discipling ministry. Barnabas had greatly influenced Paul's ministry. He had vouched for him when as Saul, newly converted, he had come to the Jerusalem church.[2] Saul, shortly thereafter had returned to his home town Tarsus.

After some time Barnabas remembered this young man and went to Tarsus to encourage Saul to join him in the church at Antioch.[3] Saul spent the next year as Barnabas' "Timothy," teaching the word and even accompanying him to Jerusalem.[4] Upon their return to Antioch, Barnabas and Saul were appointed as missionaries and sent on their first missionary trip.[5]

Leaving Antioch as a team, Barnabas being the more prominent of the two they were referred to as Barnabas and Saul. Arriving in Lystra, they were received as gods because of the healing of a crippled man, and the priests of Jupiter ascribed the name of their god to Barnabas.[6] In the beginning Barnabas' nephew Mark had also been in their company [7] but he had early on returned to Jerusalem,[8] offending Paul by his defection. From then on, Paul deemed Mark unfit for missionary service.

After Lystra things seem to change in the structure of the team. Saul's name changed to Paul and the order in which they are named is reversed. From then on they are known as Paul and Barnabas.

Following the first missionary trip Paul and Barnabas returned to Antioch where they taught the word. Then we have this record in Acts 15:35-41:

> *Paul also and Barnabas continued in Antioch, teaching and preaching the word of the Lord, with many others also.*
>
> *And some days after Paul said unto Barnabas, "Let us go again and visit our brethren in every city where we have preached the word of the Lord, and see how they do."*
>
> *And Barnabas determined to take with them John, whose surname is Mark. But Paul thought not good to take him with them, who departed from them from Pamphylia, and went not with them to the work. And the contention was so sharp between them, that they departed asunder one from the other: and so Barnabas took Mark and sailed unto Cyprus. And Paul chose Silas, and departed, being recommended by the brethren unto the grace of God. And he went through Syria and Cilicia, confirming the churches.*

Faithful Doctor Luke wrote the book of Acts just as the Holy Spirit inspired him to do, and according to the Spirit's integrity, as in all of scripture, the portraits of the characters were painted with "warts and all." Perhaps one of the chief dangers of being specifically chosen for a unique ministry and the anointing and revelation that accompanies such a calling is pride. Paul, when writing to the Corinthians said,

> *"And lest I be exalted above measure through the abun-*

dance of the revelations, there was given to me a thorn in
the flesh, the messenger of Satan to buffet me, lest I should
be exalted above measure." [9]

This is interpreted by many to mean that the problem is that
others may exalt the apostle overmuch, therefore God allowed his
affliction to curb their adulation. Probably so; but perhaps it also
served to deliver Paul from the tendency that is evident in his relationship with Barnabas. Solomon in his wisdom wrote, "*Only by
pride cometh contention.*" [10] Paul and Barnabas had contended so
sharply that they divided and, it seems, remained distant for many
years.

Barnabas' name interpreted means "the son of consolation." [11]
It was a name given him by the apostles because it apparently described his manner and his character. He gave his all for the Gospel. He was on hand to mentor the young believers and the young
churches that they comprised. He had mentored Paul, and was sent
by the apostles in Jerusalem to establish the young disciples in Antioch, and he had mentored Mark even when Paul had written him
off as a failure. Now at the end of his course, Paul, recognizing
Mark's worth to the ministry, calls for him from prison. He will
benefit from the love, time, patience and trust that "the son of consolation" poured into Paul's reject. Mark, too, went on to contribute
to the New Testament.

16 *At my first answer no man stood with me, but
all men forsook me: I pray God that it might not be
laid to their charge.* **17** *Notwithstanding the Lord
stood with me, and strengthened me; that by me the
preaching might be fully known, and that all the
Gentiles might hear: and I was delivered out of the
mouth of the lion.* **18** *And the Lord shall deliver me
from every evil work, and will preserve me unto his
heavenly kingdom: to whom be glory for ever and
ever. Amen.*

They had sailed with him on the Mediterranean, had marched with him through the cities of Asia Minor, Macedonia, Greece and Italy. They had preached the good news from Jerusalem to Yugoslavia, which was then Illyricum. But in the final confrontation with the forces of Nero they fled. It was a bitter blow. As you read his letter you can hear the disappointment in his voice and sense it in his words.

These are men Paul loved. They had done his bidding at great peril to their safety. They had left their homes and all that they owned to follow the Lord on Paul's apostolic team. Perhaps it was not over for them. God could raise them up again. He prays for them that God will not lay it to their charge. He had not prayed that way for Alexander the coppersmith who had done Paul much evil; he was an enemy of the Gospel who had greatly withstood the words of truth and of whom Timothy must beware. These, on the other hand, were men who had stumbled. I wonder if Mark's defection and the wonderful redemption he had enjoyed crossed Paul's mind. If it did, he may have thought, It's not over till it's over.

Paul escaped the fate of lesser known Christians that were fed to the lions for the entertainment of debauched and bloodthirsty spectators. He was confident that God was able to keep that which he had committed to him against that day; and that having delivered him from every evil work, he would usher him into his heavenly kingdom. Then he would pass from the jurisdiction of Nero's domain to that of King Jesus, ruler of the eternal kingdom of God, whose glory is for ever and ever.

(Endnotes)
[1] Colossians 4:14
[2] Acts 9:26-28
[3] Acts 11:22-26
[4] Acts 11:29,30
[5] Acts 13:1-3
[6] Acts 14:8-12
[7] Acts 12:25
[8] Acts 13:13
[9] 2 Corinthians 12:7
[10] Proverbs 13:10
[11] Acts 4:36

Chapter 9

Independence

The history of the early church as recorded in the book of Acts makes evident how closely the saints worked and fellowshipped together. Paul's ministry is an example of teamwork; there is coordination and authority. His apostolic team consisted of at least seven men beside Luke and Paul, whose names are recorded in Acts 20:4. Other names are also recorded throughout the Epistles and the book of Acts. These had a common goal, to evangelize the world and start churches in every place. It seems there were other apostolic teams as well, but this is the one of which we have record in the New Testament.

Paul was the man commissioned by God to lead this group of men. He sent them to various places with specific assignments and they carried out his orders. He was not only their leader, he was also their servant. The Lord Jesus had taught that the servant is no greater than his lord. He had told his disciples,

> *"Ye know that the princes of the Gentiles exercise dominion over them, and they that are great exercise authority upon them. But it shall not be so with you: but whosoever will be great among you, let him be your minister; and whosoever will be chief among you, let him be your servant: even as the Son of man came not to be ministered unto, but*

to minister, and to give his life a ransom for many."

In keeping with this instruction, while Paul's missionary team labored in Corinth, Paul took employment in the tent shop of Aquilla and Priscilla and provided for his men as they carried out their ministries. Later he said,

"I have coveted no man's silver, or gold, or apparel. Yea, ye yourselves know, that these hands have ministered unto my necessities, and to them that were with me." [1]

There was no question about Paul's commitment to the saints. He even claimed that he cared for all the churches.[2] And no wonder, he had been involved in establishing a great number of them, sealing a bond between himself and them. His home church, though, was Antioch from where he had been sent out to do his apostolic work. Even this apostle, although his ministry was wide ranging, was no lone ranger. He had not taken it upon himself to roam the world preaching the Gospel. He had been called of God, his call had been acknowledged by those in oversight of the Antioch church, and they had commissioned him to the work along with the apostle Barnabas.[3]

At the end of his career, however, he is forced to stand before his oppressors alone. Timothy, also subject to authority, must be capable of standing alone as well if need be. The saints are not normally lone rangers; they are functioning members of a body; and body members are not designed to function independently. God has set authority and order in the church, and we are to be subject to it.

The church, like an army, is designed to do battle, and warfare is its occupation. Soldiers are trained to obey orders and to keep rank. They are also trained to stand in emergencies and think on their feet. Every soldier is an army of one if need be. That is why every believer must know how to listen to the Lord and be led by the Spirit of God. Although it is stated in various ways, we know from more than one epistle that every man must bear his own burden and that each will give account of himself. The group is balanced by the individual. Cooperation is balanced by the ability to stand alone if that should become necessary.

Independence can be a bad word. On the mission field, independent missionaries are often looked upon with suspicion by those affiliated with organizations. Sometimes that suspicion is warranted because some independents are rebels against authority who went without being sent. But that is certainly not always true. Without a certain independence—being individually motivated—it is impossible to be completely subservient to the Spirit and uninfluenced by the unauthorized opinions of others. Since independence can be abused, we need to know what is meant by that word as we use it here. What is independence?

Webster says independence is,

1. freedom from support or government by others;

2. a competency or self-reliance.

Since #1 could imply shunning the cooperation or legitimate authority of others—such as elders or apostolic team leaders—that is not what we want to convey. It is #2, competency and self-reliance, the recognition of individual responsibility, influence and accountability: that is the independence demonstrated by the Lord's servant. It means relying totally upon God even while committed to functioning with other members of the body of Christ. There are many scriptural exhortations to this kind of independence.

Individual Responsibility

In Galatians chapter 6 some readers find a contradiction between Paul's command in verse 2, "*Bear ye one another's burdens,*" and his exhortation in verses 4, 5, "*But let every man prove his own work, and then shall he have rejoicing in himself alone, and not in another. For every man shall bear his own burden.*" In fact there is no contradiction, but an example of what we are calling independence.

Each of us is solely responsible to prove his own work, not relying on others to pick up the slack. We are to obey the Lord without waiting for motivation or permission from others. Bear your own burden; shoulder your obligations. But at the same time, don't watch another suffer with circumstances or struggle with trials without offering help and intercession. Remember, it is better to give than to receive.

> *"Wherefore, my beloved, as ye have always obeyed, not as in my presence only, but now much more in my absence, work out your own salvation with fear and trembling; For it is God that worketh in you both to will and to do of his good pleasure."* [4]

Some folks work well and willingly under supervision, but relax when there is no visible authority present. That is not acceptable. Paul's exhortation is to be as diligent in the absence of visible authority as you would be in its presence, in fact much more so.

Work out your own salvation is sometimes misunderstood to mean that our salvation is the result of our own efforts. Not so, *for it is God that worketh in you both to will and to do of his good pleasure*. God does the work, and he does it in you: not only in the apostle or the supervisor, but in you. The message is, work out your own salvation... because God works in *you*. This applies equally to the work of mission, or to "secular" work. *Whatever you do, do it heartily as unto the Lord and not unto men.* [5] When we do something for other men to see, when our diligence is motivated by the desire to appear diligent before men, or when we work at the level established by those around us, we are not working as unto the Lord. We are merely *acting* like faithful men. We then become actors (The Greek word for actor is "hypocrite"). We need an independent approach to obedience. Even though he is subject to and coordinated by an overseer, the servant of the Lord is independently motivated.

Individual Judgment

Every man's work will be judged. It is imperative therefore, that the servant of the Lord be aware of his personal accountability before the only judge that ultimately matters. Your ministry can be performed only by you; mine by me. No one else can relieve us of our responsibility before God. We must be individually motivated to initiate that to which God has called us in spite of the apparent lethargy, fear or outright disobedience of those around us.

Paul wrote other letters at other times to other people. Together those epistles round out his doctrine, which is still valid. It is incumbent upon every generation to recognize it as current instruction. When he wrote to Corinth he implied that every person in Christ is building upon the foundation that has been laid.

> *"According to the grace of God which is given unto me, as a wise master builder, I have laid the foundation, and another buildeth thereon. But let every man take heed how he buildeth thereupon. For other foundation can no man lay than that is laid, which is Jesus Christ. Now if any man build upon this foundation gold, silver, precious stones, wood hay, stubble; every man's work shall be made manifest: for the day shall declare it, because it shall be revealed by fire; and the fire shall try every man's work of what sort it is. If any man's work abide which he hath built thereupon, he shall receive a reward. If any man's work shall be burned, he shall suffer loss: but he himself shall be saved; yet so as by fire."* [6]

This admonition is addressed to every man, indicating that all are builders in this ever-growing body of Christ. The warning is that if any man build upon this foundation, whatever quality material he uses, the day shall declare it, because it will be tried with fire to reveal what sort it is. The question is not how much, but what sort. Whatever the sort, be sure it will pass through the fire on the day that God judges it.

What can we make of these words: "any man," "every man's work," "he shall suffer loss," "he shall receive a reward?" These are words about individuals, not groups or organizations. The work of every man will be tried and judged independently. Every individual will be rewarded or suffer loss independent of everyone else. Since this is the case, how could it be more important that every faithful man recognize his personal responsibility to obey the Lord regardless of what others around him may do?

Individually Gifted

God has distributed gifts and ministries to individual members of the body.

> *"But the manifestation of the Spirit is given to every man to profit withal. For to one is given by the Spirit the word of wisdom; to another the word of knowledge by the same Spirit; to another faith by the same Spirit; to another the gifts of healing by the same Spirit; to another the working of miracles; to another prophecy; to another discerning of spirits; to another divers kinds of tongues; to another interpretation of tongues: but all these worketh that one and selfsame Spirit, dividing to every man severally as he will."* [7]

Once again the object of God's giving is every man. "Given to every man," "to one is given," "to another is given." There is no special class of people that God chooses through which to manifest the Spirit. This portion of scripture ends with, "...*the selfsame Spirit dividing to every man severally as he will*." If God endues every believer separately according to his will, each individual is responsible to minister those gifts on the occasion of God's direction. Paul understood that and obeyed the Lord; sometimes at his own peril. His desire is that Timothy embrace that same independent obedience and, projecting ahead, that you and I be as responsive to God's leading.

As a young believer I experienced a situation that illustrated Paul's words. It also embarrassed me and instructed me about individual, independent response to God's direction. Having been saved only a short time I was not confident that God could move in me as in any other believer. I was sitting one day with a pastor and a visiting evangelist. Also present was the pastor's wife and his infant son. The baby was sick, and as his father held him he seemed to be growing rapidly more feverish. Someone suggested that we pray for the boy; so we did.

As the others prayed, I felt a strong urge to lay hands on the baby and pray for him. I reasoned that I had never done anything like that before, and here were two ministers that probably had; for some reason I felt afraid and embarrassed, so I didn't do it. After they had prayed there was no change in the baby's condition. I, a little confused and troubled that I hadn't obeyed, went out and walked while the Holy Spirit convicted me of my disobedience.

After enduring for a while an increasingly unbearable struggle within myself, I felt compelled to return to the house. By this time the men were gone, but the mother was there, and the child lay on the couch burning with fever. With difficulty I sheepishly confessed to the pastor's wife what I had experienced and how I had disobeyed. She told me they had all been aware of that at the time, and that it would be good if I would do it now. I knelt beside the baby, laid my hand on his forehead, confessed my disobedience to the Lord and asked him to heal the child. Immediately I felt the heat of the fever travel up my arm, the flush left the boy's face and within minutes he was well.

I have never claimed a gift of healing based on this incident, nor has God used me often in this manner. This experience helped me to understand that the manifestation of the Spirit is given to every member of the body, and He divides to every man severally as He will. There are men who are specifically gifted as we see in other portions of scripture, but He can use any one of us to perform His will at any given time. It is His work, His power, and His choice. It may never be known how many tragedies might have been averted or how much rejoicing there may have been instead of sorrow if individual believers had not waited for someone else to take the initiative in something God had urged them to do.

In this same chapter Paul wrote,

> *"Now ye are the body of Christ, and members in particular."* [8]

Each of us is a body member for whom there is no substitute, therefore we cannot wait for someone else to initiate what God has told us to do.

Independently Accountable

In the light of what has been said about the bearing of our own burdens, the working out of our own salvation, the testing of every man's works and the individual gifting of body members, let us be aware that we are also individually accountable.

> *"So then every one of us shall give account of himself to God,"* [9]

Someday we shall each stand before the judgment seat of Christ to receive judgment or reward *for the works done in our bodies whether they be good or bad.* [10] In that day none of us will be able to excuse himself by claiming his lethargy or disobedience was caused by someone else. God will require an accounting of why we were not willing to obey when He spoke to us individually.

One day it will be the last day. The last trumpet will sound, we shall be changed [11] and called to give account.[12] Perhaps some of us are busy with things that seem important, but are unrelated to the will of God; in fact the will of God was not even considered when we undertook them. As saints we must realize that there are no exceptions when God's word says "every man." Even if that last day—the day of the trumpet—should be many days, years, or even generations beyond our time, every one of us will experience that day of accounting at the end of our short life span. Three times in the last chapter of The Revelation Jesus said, *"I come quickly."*

> *"And behold, I come quickly, and my reward is with me, to give every man according as his work shall be. I am Alpha and Omega, the beginning and the end, the first and the last...surely I come quickly."* [13]

And the apostle John's response was,

> *"Amen. Even so, come, Lord Jesus."*

"Thanks be to God, which giveth us the victory through our Lord Jesus Christ. Therefore, my beloved brethren, be ye steadfast, unmovable, always abounding in the work of the Lord, forasmuch as ye know that your labor is not in vain in the Lord." [14]

19 Salute Prisca and Aquila,and the household of Onesiphorus. 20 Erastus abode at Corinth: but Trophimus have I left at Miletum sick. 21 Do thy diligence to come before winter. Eubulus greeteth thee, and Pudens, and Linus, and Claudia, and all the brethren. 22 The Lord Jesus Christ be with thy spirit. Grace be with you. Amen.

THE END

(Endnotes)

[1] Acts 20: 33,34
[2] 2 Corinthians 11:28
[3] Acts 13:1-4
[4] Philippians 2:12,13
[5] Colossians 3:17,23
[6] 1 Corinthians 3:10-15
[7] 1 Corinthians 12:7-11
[8] 1 Corinthians 12:27
[9] Romans 14:12
[10] 2 Corinthians 5:10; Colossians 3:24,25
[11] 1 Corinthians 15:50
[12] Romans 14:12
[13] Revelation 22:12,13,20
[14] 1 Corinthians 15:57,58